The Treasure Within Us

Sofia Adamova

The Treasure Within Us First published in 2009 by;

Ecademy Press

6, Woodland Rise, Penryn, Cornwall, UK. TR10 8QD

info@ecademy-press.com

www.ecademy-press.com

Cover Design and Typesetting by Charlotte Mouncey in Warnock pro 12pt on 16pt

Printed and Bound by; Lightning Source in the UK and USA

Printed on acid-free paper from managed forests.

This book is printed on demand, so no copies will be remaindered or pulped.

ISBN 978-1-905823-46-8

To my mum.
You showed me The Way
without knowing that...
Always love you.

Contents

Foreword

I have a message to share, which means so much to me. I know some of us are so self-obsessed that we don't notice what is happening around us. I have been quite lucky so far, having a lot of free time and being able to choose what I want to do in my life. That is, I guess, my number one value - freedom of choice. We all live according to our values, what is important to us. I have been watching people, whenever I am on a bus going on my favourite route or in a crowd in Portobello market or in a conference listening to discussions about the current situation in the economy. I never stopped wondering, why these people are living their lives the way they do. I was trying to guess what it is on their mind, what they hide behind that smile, or why they look tired and unhappy. We know we are all unique with different experiences, different circumstances and different lives. But at the same time we are all human beings, and that is what unites us, makes us a part of the whole.

So, I am always sitting there and wondering, maybe I could make this person happier, make him think differently; help him to discover the treasure within himself. Because we all know the answers, but it is like owning the ocean, though it contains the whole underwater world it is sometimes not easy to find things there, unless you know where to look! How do we know how to be in the right place at the right time? How do we attune ourselves to the frequency that has the answer to that particular question? Do we really need to know everything? Or is there a much simpler way?

We have had so many theories and recipes for how to be happy, some easy, some really complicated. But what really works? Again, there is no wrong answer, it depends on the individual. The secret is, there is no shortcut, no easy way. It will take some time. Yes, you might have heard that change can be instant, that is very true. However, just to make the program work will still take some time, even if we created the change in a heartbeat.

We are today what we designed in our minds some time ago. We are the product of our own thoughts and actions. It all sounds easy but as we know, genius is in simplicity.

The reason you hold this book is not pure chance, nothing happens by chance in this world. It means you are ready to move to the next level, see beyond the horizon, break the boundaries of the box you created, start living a fuller life, living your purpose.

"Just imagine that we all have this little chest inside us with different codes. In our hectic lives we sometimes forget about its existence. That is when we start being unhappy, lose control over our own lives, get confused and feel that we are going in the wrong direction. All we need to do is to open the chest and reprogram it, set our goal, and design the future we desire most. Because the way our life is now, is the very way we programmed our tiny treasure chest some time ago."

So let us set off on a journey of discovery of ourselves, to the very depth of the ocean of our individual world and find the treasure of our life.

Section 1: The Magic Wheel. The Components of Balanced Life.

Our life wouldn't be complete if we lacked one of the axes. These are vital components of our life. On the scale from 1 to 10 where are you in each area of your life? Is your wheel absolutely round or does it have sharp angles? What is the main area you need to work on? How balanced is your life at the moment? The next few chapters will guide you through all the constituents and will help you to determine which area of your life needs most assistance and how you are going to make it work.

1.1. Health Is Beauty.

"Every human being is the author of his own health or disease".
Hindu Prince Gautama Siddhartha,
the founder of Buddhism,
563-483 B.C.

We all consider health to be the main issue in our life. Sometimes we even say that if we had better health we would excel in that particular field or achieve our goals more easily. We believe good health is either a gift or something you inherit. We think that to be healthy we need to do things you don't enjoy. As Mark Twain said, 'The only way to keep your health is to eat what you don't want, drink what you don't like and do what you'd rather not.'

We trust our doctors and the pills they prescribe. We spend thousands of pounds on our medical insurance because we expect to get ill. We blame the NHS for not providing us with decent service. We rely on science and expect revolutionary new medicine to cure new fatal, incurable diseases. We tell ourselves THEY are in charge of how we are going to feel tomorrow. We blame pollution, or the quality of food, or just something else. What is it all about then? Is it the truth or just our belief system? Who is in control of our health and our life? It is only we who can decide that!

I was lucky to be born in a family where my mum believed we were responsible for our own health. That was the time when we had sometimes to wait for up to five hours in a queue to see a doctor. The service was free but very basic. And she couldn't afford to have a private doctor. My parents had three children under ten years old, and they were still in their twenties. My mum decided that she could change it. I remember when I was twelve our family suddenly became vegetarian. And because it was my mum who was cooking we had to obey the new 'rules'. I used to sneak with my sisters to see our grandma and she would cook some really nice pork for us. Two years later my mum changed her mind and we went back to 'normal' diet. Everybody was happy. But because we lived not far from the seacoast we would generally have more fish than meat and also we raised our own chickens, so we rarely bought any meat from the market. My dad was also a very keen hunter and we would have lots of game. We all had very good health and hardly had to see a doctor.

When I was nineteen I was chosen to go to Cyprus for an internship from our university, which was exactly what I was dreaming of! We stayed in a beautiful house with a swimming pool. Everything was paid for us. But it was very hard work and it was extremely hot. We all had to eat what was cooked for us in the hotel and as the food wasn't too much to my liking, we used to nick some cakes and sweets from the main restaurant. By the end of the six-month placement some girls gained up to 30 pounds. I was about 15 pounds heavier. I hated work and was very unhappy. It was the first time in my life I was away from home for such a long time. Now I was cut off the rest of the world and even my new, first ever mobile phone was stolen one month after I bought it!

One day I was working in the main bar and got poisoned with schnitzel at lunchtime. I felt horrible, I could hardly walk and I think I turned green! All I could think of was to go home, take a pill and just lie down. But we were really busy at that time and the manager didn't let me go home! Maybe I should have insisted but for some reason I continued to work. I was fine next day, but I decided for myself that I wouldn't eat meat again. At that time it wasn't a decision based just on the fact I got poisoned. I wanted to take control. I knew about the harm that meat does to your body from when I was very young. I knew that eating too much meat could lead to heart disease or a stroke, because it contains saturated fats which raise your cholesterol level. I knew meat can poison you and we had a few epidemics in our country, especially from exported beef or chicken. But like everybody else, I didn't care a lot because I didn't see the results of damage straight away. This is where our flawed perceptions come from! We feel good straight away after eating a hamburger but we don't see what happens to our body because it takes time. At home we would never have so much meat and when we had it, no more than twice a week, it was always organic. It's been nearly five years since that summer and I am really happy I took that decision! The main thing is, I never missed steak or a ham sandwich! Because I didn't just give up eating meat (and you know what happens when you try to give up something you really enjoy, you start craving it), it never happened to me. This was because the change occurred in my mind first. I stopped associating meat with something edible. I still enjoy fish and seafood a lot because I believe it is good for me, but I never ever wanted meat again! Changing my mindset took me literally a second. Giving up something just for the sake of it can take you months or even years. You know some people who tried giving up smoking and then a few years later went back to their old habit.

So how is it possible? You can use this skill for giving up any other bad habits. Like smoking, drugs, alcohol, eating junk food or just overeating!

Perhaps some of you are thinking now, 'Oh, you just need to be determined to do that and have a very strong will.' Yes, this is the hardest way. It will make you suffer a lot and you will stop enjoying your life for a while! I tried this option before when I was dieting. I would just eat three apples and drink two cups of coffee a day. I called it '5 Star diet', because it always contained no more than five meals a day. I could have fewer apples and more coffee. Fruit would provide me with essential vitamins and fibre and caffeine would boost my energy level. And then I would escape to a secluded bank of the river where nobody could disturb me and there wouldn't be any smell of food. And I could stay there the whole day, having a swim against the current for exercise every couple of hours. The whole experience was never easy. I felt hungry most of the day, especially the hours between 3 and 6 pm. But I felt so happy every day when I went to bed, because I knew next morning I would be a few pounds lighter! After three to four days I would lose up to 7 - 8 pounds and would look and feel great.

And guess what would happen next?

In about two weeks time I would gain it all back.

Now I eat everything I want, I never diet, never starve myself and keep a desirable weight! How can that be real, you will ask? To have a great body you need to suffer! What's the secret? Is there any? Yes, there is. It is the same secret I used to stop eating meat so easily. It is the same secret you can use to stop smoking or to cure a disease. Because, believe me, you have all the resources you need to do that! It is not about paying an enormous sum of money or going for expensive treatment or waiting for a miracle from scientists! It is all in your head. Yes, in your head.

We all have a perception of ourselves. We all 'know' who we are and what is 'good' or 'bad' for us. We love other people's opinion and trust their advice more than ourselves! We will argue over beliefs with other people to prove 'our' point. Because we 'heard it on TV'! We will let other people tell us what to do and that makes us feel looked after. Because we love that feeling of comfort and we are ready to pay the price for it. What if somebody told you that succumbing to all these beliefs would cost you hundreds of thousands of pounds, that you will only enjoy your life 50% of its potential and would shorten your life span by at least 10%? But of course, nobody would ever tell you. The thing is - you can stop doing that right now. It is like paying a bad solicitor just because you don't know the law! And let him ruin your life and steal your savings! Now it is time for you to decide if you want to 'go with the flow' or get behind the wheel? Do you want to be in control or be controlled? Do you want to be healthy and happy?

There is a very easy technique, but it is like a software programme – the more you use it, the better you understand it and the easier it is to operate it. It contains a few essential steps.

- Set your standards higher. Don't be happy with what you have –you don't have to put up with circumstances, you can create a better environment around you!

- Make a decision based on your higher standards. (I want to be slim and toned, because I would feel and look so much better!)

- Desire it. Feel it with every cell of your body. Imagine yourself how you will look like if you achieve your goal.

- Imagine yourself as a white piece of canvas. Absolutely clean. This is a body. It doesn't matter for now if you don't find your body that ideal. There is no link between you and a canvas. It is you. Then imagine it is a warm sunny day and you are standing on a terrace of a beautiful house by the river (wherever you feel happy) with a brush and set of paints. Your mind is the mind of an artist. And you are about to paint something absolutely amazing on this crisp white canvas! ANYTHING you want! Because you are the artist, right? What are you going to paint there? Every stroke of a brush is a small story. How do you want to look? To feel? To be? Once you decide to accept only the best from the best, you start thinking of yourself in a different way.

- So, next step, TAKE this decision! The magic thing is you don't have to tell other people about it. There is no need- they will see it on your picture! People will pause in front of your painting to admire it! You don't have to tell them how beautiful your picture is because our perception of beauty is quite similar to each other's. And people will start changing around you. You will be amazed how contagious it is! After I became vegetarian, three months later my sister stopped eating meat! I never told her anything! I never tried to convince her!

- The next thing will happen to you at a subconscious level, so you might not recognise it straight away. You will start to understand your body language and read the secret signals it gives you all the time. It might take time to develop, but be patient! Our body knows everything! It knows what it needs to cure a disease or how to get rid of toxins (which we might have no idea of at a conscious level!) You don't need to read hundreds of books in order to figure out what is the 'right' diet for you. You might need some guidance at the beginning until you become confident enough with your new skill to carry on by yourself. The signals will be very subtle at first – you will feel like eating one particular dish or fruit. I am sure you get these signals now but they come from a different mindset, so you can't rely on them until you acquire a new one. So if you are craving crisps, the signal comes from a mindset like this, 'I like crisps because they make me feel good. All my friends eat crisps. We all have crisps while watching TV and I don't really care if I gain a pound or two. Anyway - I eat lots of other junk food so eating some crisps won't make any difference. Maybe one day. I am not that fat yet / I am fat anyway. It is so hard to resist them. I just want to relax and enjoy my life. What is the reason to be here if not to have fun?' And that is what you get! Our desires are the commands of our mind.

Not any more. You want it to be a beautiful picture people will look at, holding their breath. If you are a parent I am sure you want your kids to be healthy. And banning particular food at home won't help much if is not what they want! You should never push it too hard. Forbidden fruit is the most desirable! But changing the culture of having meals at home can make a huge difference!

When you imagine yourself as a white new canvas you don't want to spoil it with an 'inappropriate' stroke of the brush! How can you possibly stain your beautiful clean body with some junk food? It might taste great but after you swallow it you will feel totally disgusted! If you have a bowl of fresh salad and spend an hour in a gym – believe me, you will feel very happy with yourself. At the same time it means that if you really want something you can have it of course, and when it is not forbidden it is less desirable. And drop these common beliefs that salad is 'rabbit food'. People made it up to justify their junk eating habits! You don't want to support their 'party' any more. You are in control now!

We are all different and there is no one specific diet we should all stick to all year round. The best way to find out is to go to the supermarket when you are NOT hungry. This is very important because when your body doesn't need immediate satisfaction it will react in a different way when choosing the food. Just go slowly along the shelves and listen to your body. You will be amazed what kind of food it can desire! Once you learn how to read your body signals you will automatically pick up all the right food! Sometimes you will feel like having some pasta and then maybe your body won't want it for weeks! For me it is always lots of fresh salad and tomatoes. Lately I've been crazy about goat cheese. Sometimes my body gives me signals that I eat too much protein and I suddenly stop wanting fish and seafood. Our body can't store protein and if you eat more than you need you'll eliminate it through urine, putting an extra strain on your kidneys to metabolize it. But I don't need to know the theory, my body sends me the signal and it all happens naturally. Cutting back on your meat and fatty unhealthy food intake will reduce certain health risks but you might not notice the physical benefits for a while. However you will get a sense of mental satisfaction out of sticking with a dietary change because you know you are improving your health little by little.

When I mastered reading my body signals I found myself leaving half a portion of food in a restaurant and saying no to a glass of beer or wine when I didn't really want it. Or having a cake! Yes! Because there is no food you can never ever eat again. You can treat yourself and your body knows when to tell you to stop. And without ever dieting and starving yourself again you suddenly find yourself losing weight, signing for membership at a gym and being generally happier. It feels so great that you KNOW even if you can't really explain what it is.

Another way we can improve our health and in particular, heal our body is using the power of thought. We have tremendous potential inside us to create miracles in our life and heal incurable diseases.

Psychologist Rivil Kofman saved herself from cancer, and then puzzled out the secret of fatal disease. She started helping children to overcome it. And, surprisingly, an imaginary world, in which children saw their healing, started to become reality. Just like with the help of little "rescuers", affected cells were built again. Oncologists call Kofman's method fairy tale therapy. It works as a complement to traditional medicine, making it stronger. More than 500 children with cancer were cured with her help.

When Rivil was in her fifth month of pregnancy, doctors discovered cancer in her. She was told that her fourth baby could die, and she simply wouldn't be able to survive the delivery. "I didn't even think of another option and decided to give birth." The baby was born healthy. But mum got an infection during the transfusion of blood. She started losing her sight and hearing. After a long examination doctors gave her the diagnosis - combined sclerosis. And – a growing tumour.

"I was saved by one American boy," she recalls. "He told me a secret, which helped me to survive. This boy had cancer. Every day he imagined he was shooting his tumour with a toy pistol, imagining cancer as a big monster. I realised the secret is not in that, it is all about love, you have to love your disease." She asked doctors to draw a scheme of her illness. They explained to her in detail how and in what time disease affects the body and how the nerve endings stop functioning. "One morning I woke up and couldn't move my leg, I thought, which of the nerve endings died? So I decided that I was going to build my body from the beginning." Rivil believed that thoughts materialise. Every morning and night she drew in her imagination a "building project". Joyful workers, dressed in colourful suits restored her organism. At last Rivil managed to make a few steps, then more, then she started walking again. That was

a victory! She worked out the secret, so she couldn't forget about it and realised she needed to take it out to people.

Her first pupils were children with cancer. Rivil would go to the hospitals and meet kids who were considered "hopeless". Rivil made a fairy costume and went to Mariopul to meet a little boy called Egor. His mother, choking with tears, begged her to help. Cancer had got to the last stage. Egor had chemotherapy but his condition was getting worse. Rivil made up a fairy tale with him. "Barakaballa is a small cancer cell, which came to us from another planet. She got lost in the shop and got into a body of a small boy. It was just necessary to love her, so she could return to her planet." The boy believed the story and was healed.

Rivil realised that there is nothing impossible if you believe you can make it. Full of joy, as if she was made of light, she doesn't like talking about sad things. She is dreaming of her own theatre, where she can heal thousands of children with fairy tales.

So now, when you have decided you want to be effortlessly healthy (I say 'effortlessly' but it may take time for you to get to the state where all you do will only bring you pleasure and satisfaction) we can help you with some guidance. Or feel free to refer to our website www.thetreasurecompanies.co.uk for a free consultation or more information on this topic.

Write down what you 'know' is good and not really good for you concerning the way you treat your body. Take a pen, relax, listen to yourself...and then note it down.

Watch your behaviour change for the next couple of weeks and then write down what has changed in your food preferences. Then do the same in 2-3 months time. How do people around you react? Have they changed their habits? How do you feel?

Health

1.2. Personal Relationships.

She was only sixteen when they met. He was charming, good looking and generous. And twelve years older, married with two kids. They felt attracted to each other straight away. She stopped going to college and was living from one date to another. He would buy her presents and promise to leave his family and marry her. After two and a half years, lots of happy moments and tears of frustration, he went to Germany for a few weeks. He never came back. He secretly moved his family to Germany and kept on promising to come back very soon. It was two more years before the girl gave up and started looking around.

Another story.

She was seventeen and he was nineteen. They had been seeing each other for a year before they decided to get married. It was a spectacular wedding with lots of guests and presents. She just gave a birth to a beautiful girl a few months ago. The couple is very happy and now planning a second baby.

There are millions of stories like this. Relationships determine how you get on in your life. And it is not just people we date and marry, in business you hear every day that, "it is all about relationships". They shape our lives; they impact on our mood, our career, our business.

What is the secret of getting and maintaining exceptional relationships? How do you attract the right person into your life? There are plenty of ways of meeting and attracting new people in our lives: you can go out every night, spend hours in bars hoping somebody will offer you a drink, smile at your gym instructors, flirt with your colleagues, the list can go forever... And still you can be alone and feeling extremely lonely. In order for magic to happen your thoughts, words, actions and surroundings must be congruent with your desires. Just know it will happen - behave as it is already in your life and be patient. The universe loves rewarding those who can wait.

One of the most wonderful examples of this is a story of a man who divorced his wife in his mid-forties. He wanted to start a 'second life' and attract his perfect partner into his life. He had done all the right things: he knew what qualities she should have; he knew how he wanted her to be and even visualized her in his life. Despite doing all those things – nothing happened. And he started losing confidence that he could fall in love again. His friends tried to help him and introduced him to a few women. But relationships didn't last long.

Then, one night, he had a dream. He was in the forest, right in the middle of a sunlit meadow. He felt very relaxed and happy. He suddenly knew that no matter how hard he tried - nothing would happen until he let things happen at their natural pace. He trusted his inner feelings and stopped worrying and waiting. He accepted the fact he didn't have a partner at the moment but he knew he wasn't lonely –he had a wonderful family and lots of friends. He just let his impatience go. A few weeks after he had the dream he got a call from a neighbour, who was running a beauty salon. She invited him to a party with her friends and among them there was a single girl, who was her good client. He said he wasn't interested. A few days later the girl called him herself. They spent over two hours on the phone and next morning he brought her coffee in bed. They got married a month later...

When you know she is the one, there is no point waiting. But it was worth waiting for her to appear in his life.

Meeting your partner is only one part of the story. We get so excited and happy when we are falling in love. And what happens next? How can such a nice loving person turn into a selfish, careless man or woman? Why couldn't we see it before? The reason is, it is still the very same person and it was no coincidence we met him or her. That was a Divine Order and we are here to learn those lessons and when the time comes we should just move on. If you think something is wrong with your relationship because you feel sad and frustrated at some times – you are missing out the bigger picture, because this is the way it is designed. Your relationships with others are simply reflections of your own relationship with yourself. Unless you love yourself first, you can't truly give love to anybody else. You need to feel good about yourself first - on every subject - including health, wealth, and love. Look for the positive things in You.

But what shall we do if no matter how hard we try – it still doesn't work? You feel the love has gone and you no longer feel the same way? Maybe you have been in this relationship for a long time and you feel you have obligations now but no courage to change things? Or maybe you know that you have changed or you both have changed and nothing connects you any longer the same way as before? Or maybe it is not challenging enough? You have your own reason perhaps. Ask yourself – am I happy in my current relationship? If not, what can I do to make it work? Do I want it to work? And if you arrive at the conclusion that it would be better to change your life and leave your partner, then I encourage you to do so. Don't listen to your "caring" friends or worry about what other people might think. That is their life and this is yours. And you are the only person who knows what is better for you. Because we love listening to a piece of "good advice", even if it doesn't work out we have somebody to blame. Take responsibility for your actions. You are the most important person in your life and nobody cares more for you as yourself. Remember – you cannot make mistakes - whatever decision you take - it is the right one.

Another reason so many stay in unhealthy relationships is because they think it will not be fair to their children to have separated parents or they are horrified about the idea of sharing their assets. What they really do is they postpone the decision to the time when they won't able to bear this relationship any longer and by that time it might have a worse effect on the whole family. Or they might never do it and miss out on wonderful opportunities, continuing to live miserable unhappy lives.

To make this kind of decision takes some courage. But hey, your happiness and probably the happiness of your loved ones are at stake! Isn't it worth it? I don't encourage you to make hasty (inconsiderate) decisions. I only encourage you to take a first step to living a more fulfilled, purposeful life. And you deserve it!

Anyway, the choice is always yours. Trust your feelings, because you know what you really should do. Listen to your heart. Take your time. Life is always this way. It is full of contradictions. Nothing is forever and at the same time – the universe is eternal, it is the same matter as it was millions years ago, only constantly changing shapes and form. People will come into your life and go at some point. We can't keep anybody forever unless it is meant to be. Acknowledge how lucky you are having all these different experiences and just accept it and let it be. Remember that everything happening to you at the moment is what you created with your own thoughts some time ago. Maybe not even in this life. But it is always for the best. And the universe will show you why, just be patient.

> *"When you realize that nothing is lacking,*
> *the whole world belongs to you!"*
> Lao Tzu.

1.3. Wisdom of Character.

"A man's character is his fate".

Heraclitus c. 540-c. 480 BC

Our character is the particular combination of qualities that makes us a particular type of person. It is the unique set of those qualities that makes us different from other people. It is amazing how this blend of qualities and features shape our everyday life! Look around yourself - the place you live in, design of your room, your furniture, decorations, pictures on the walls, the clothes and fragrance you wear, the food you had for breakfast today, the programs you are watching on TV, the way you spend your time and money, the people you are surrounded with, the shops you go to, the car you drive, your hobbies and interests – what does it say about you? Your outer world is just the reflection of your inner self, the "stuff' you are really made of, the true You designed by You. And there is no other person on earth exactly like you!

So, you might think, if it is my world and it is the reflection of my unique qualities, can I by changing my qualities transform my surroundings? Absolutely. It is like cooking a soup. You can use your favourite recipe every single day of your life and your soup will taste the same! But if you change the ingredients - sometimes even one - you create a completely different taste, a different experience. There is no right or wrong. Though you might end up with a more delicious soup. It is the same with your life – change the set of your qualities and get a different outcome. This might take some time, because wisdom is something you gain through experience.

The qualities of your character can be divided in 3 categories:

- Genetic - which are defined by the arrangement of genes passed to you,

- Imprinted in your childhood - at the time when we are most receptive to things and in most cases it happens subconsciously,

- Learned or gained - qualities we are aware of, our conscious choice.

For example, smoking can be all three. If one of our parents smokes we have about 50% chance to get an addiction. If our parents smoked in our presence when we were kids, we might have perceived that as "normal" and that can influence our behaviour in the future. Or we started smoking as an adult because we found it easier to relax after a cigarette.

Another trait of character – generosity – is mostly something we learn. Either we observed our parents helping other people or maybe we had brothers and sisters and were used to sharing or we realized the importance of sharing in our grown up life. It could be some friends making donations to charities that influenced us or reading an article about poverty in third world countries or even coming across people in need in real life.

The great thing about it is that you can decide and choose which qualities you like and want to keep and which qualities you want to change or replace. Great tools, such as NLP (Neuro-Linguistic Programming), can help you get rid of habits and beliefs about yourself in no time, if you are ready to let them go. Some other qualities (such as your image, your weight, skills in a particular subject) will take more time to change. But as the saying goes - the best time to plant a tree is 20 years ago, the second best —is *now.*

I guess you know which qualities work for you and which don't. Start working with your habits. Usually it is something we know about ourselves or are being constantly told about or even being known for!

Have another look at your life, your surroundings. What is it that you are really happy with? Maybe it is your style, your circle of friends or the car you drive. Or maybe you are really proud of your job or the position you hold or maybe you are known for being always on time, Great! Make the list, put in as many qualities as you can. Praise yourself. Because you deserve it! Then look at the qualities you put down one at a time and think about how it became important to you or how it got into your life. Think about how much time it took you to acquire it and what the benefits are of having it in your life.

You might be surprised at your next exercise. Now you have to do the same with your partner's qualities. What will you put in their list? Do you see any connections? Maybe some qualities you learned from each other. And perhaps some qualities are the ones you want to have on your list!

My qualities	My partner's qualities

_____   _____

_____   _____

_____   _____

_____   _____

_____   _____

_____   _____

_____   _____

_____   _____

_____   _____

_____   _____

Limiting qualities

_____   _____

_____   _____

_____   _____

_____   _____

_____   _____

_____   _____

_____   _____

_____   _____

_____   _____

_____   _____

The next step would be to write down all the qualities that you think are limiting you, make you unhappy or make other people cross with you. Be honest. Some traits of your character you might be not aware of. This is a perfect moment to find out what they are. You can ask your close friend or your partner to help you by giving you some support and feedback. But remember - whatever they say - it is just the way *they* perceive you, it is their opinion about you and not who you are. This exercise can get a bit difficult, especially if information you get from other people is not what you expected or a total surprise for you! Be prepared to hear something you will not like. Do not try to defend yourself or argue! It is all about getting insight on things we are not aware of. Instead - be grateful, acknowledge it was helpful and thank the person.

This exercise can get even deeper, but we will stop at this stage. It is better to go through all the stages with a professional coach. For now you have enough information and hopefully can see a clearer picture of what is already present in your life. Now, ask yourself - am I happy with that? Is there anything I want to change, to improve, to get rid of in my life now? Which qualities don't I want to have any more and which ones do I want to replace them with?

If, for example, you have procrastination on your list of qualities you want to eliminate from your life and in your list of desired qualities you have immediate action, you can start by asking yourself - what stops me from starting acting now instead of postponing things all the time? Think about how much easier your life would be if you replaced one with another. If you think you don't have enough leverage to change it on your own - turn to an expert in this field - a coach or a NLP practitioner or you can talk about it to a friend of yours and get new insights, perhaps.

It might be a bit challenging and time consuming but remember -you are creating the Ideal-Self, you are designing your life and your destiny, so take the first step, think about how a tiny change in you can affect your relationships, your surroundings, your life and the lives of people you care about, the world itself. Isn't it worth it after all?

> *"When we long for life without difficulties, remind us that oaks grow strong in contrary winds and diamonds are made under pressure."*
>
> Peter Marshall

1.4. Financial Acumen.

Definition of Wealth.

What is it wealth? First of all let's look at wealth as something which is not a material gain, but a state of mind. It doesn't matter what your current financial situation is, what challenges you might be facing or what problems you had in the past. Wherever you are now, however much or little you have in your bank account at the moment, you can change your financial future today.

So if wealth is a state of mind, how shall we start thinking in order to attract abundance in our life? True wealth lies in your power to accept and give back into the flow of prosperity. The more we are able to take and the more we are ready to share determine how rich we are. Imagine if you were given a million pounds today, what would you do with the money? It is probably fairly easy. What about 10? 100 million pounds? You might have a problem at this point, because to be able to accept 100 million the capacity of your mind should match your ability to deal with such an amount of money. Do you know that people who win millions on the lottery usually end up in debt a few years later? Wealth and money are two really different things. You can use your skills to earn money, but to create wealth you need to master the art of it. Wealth is permanent, like a garden full of flowers, money is temporary like bees that come and go. But if you have a garden, you will always attract bees. Of course it will take time to plant and grow your garden, to tend to the trees and guard it from bad weather and birds. But then you will have an amazing crop of fruit and buzzing from beetles and bees.

Wealth also is a constant flow of energy surrounding us. There are trillions of pounds being transferred around the world every single day. All you need is just tap into this flow!

Your relationship with money.

What do you think of, when you think of being rich? What do you imagine? Is it limousines and exclusive suites, beautiful big houses, holidays in the Bahamas and private jets? Do you think you deserve it? Because if you do not accept the idea that you deserve abundance in your life your limiting belief will bar you from wealth. Even when prosperity comes into your life unexpectedly you still won't be able to take it!

A friend of mine inherited a villa in South of France from his aunt who died in a car accident. It was very sudden and a big surprise for everybody - first, because his aunt was still in her 40s, secondly – they never got on very well and really had any contact at all. He got so excited, I remember him saying, "I don't believe it! It can't be true. I never get anything for free!" He didn't feel he deserved it. A month later his own house was destroyed in a fire and it turned out it wasn't insured. So he punished himself by not accepting the wealth.

We have a natural ability to increase whatever we concentrate on – whether it is our money or happy moments in our relationship. If you want more abundance into your life, make space for it, expand your potential, learn to accept. Letting go and giving is another way to attract wealth into your life. The more you are happy with what you have, the more you will be able to attract into your reality.

Now it is time for a small exercise. Get a blank sheet of paper or use the space below and write the answers to the following questions.

How much money would you like to have? (Make it a definite figure.)

How would you spend your time once you have that money?

Who would you spend it with?

What would you do in your everyday life?

What are the first things you would spend your fortune on?

What is prosperity for you?

_____

_____

_____

_____

_____

To me, true prosperity is about doing things you love doing in your life, to have absolute freedom to choose what to do. It is never an amount of money- it is always a state of mind. You might be surprised when you look at your answers that they are not that much different from reality. If it true for you - my congratulations –you are already rich! But if you are not as rich as you would like to be - there is something you don't know.

Power of thought.

To attract money, you need to focus on wealth. Not on what is lacking in your life (I don't have enough), but on what you already possess. Think rich thoughts. Imagine yourself being already rich. Make yourself believe you already have the money you want. Forget the words "I can't afford". Take it out of your vocabulary forever!

Warren Buffet, the most successful investor of all times, was once asked, "How have things changed for you now that you have incredible wealth? He responded, "Well, I can afford anything I want..." Then he paused before adding, "...but then again, I always could."

Even before Buffet had actually created the wealth he enjoys today, he already had the mindset of wealth –and therefore was able to create it, because he saw the world in those terms. What we see is what we get. If it is wealth and freedom we choose - we will only have more of that. If it is lack and misery – you will attract more of that in your life.

What are our thoughts? If you could look at your body under the most powerful microscope you would see that it consists of energy and information, not solid matter. This energy and information is just a tiny bit of infinite fields of energy and information in the universe. Our body only appears solid, but if we could break what seems to be matter down into molecules and atoms and even further than that, we would realise that atom is more than 99,9999 percent empty space and the subatomic particles moving at the speed of light are actually bundles of vibrating energy. These chaotic movements of energy only seem to be random - they carry information. So by thinking different thoughts we are able to change those vibrations and therefore affect the outcome.

Start paying attention to what you think about and how you think about it. Because even if you think that your thoughts are not visible and it doesn't matter what you think as long as you say and do the "right" things, remember that we have only explored five senses so far and those are not enough to decode such information. But the universe has no such limitations and it is only us, people who carry the mask, who ensure we don't see everything.

Let's just assume for a moment that it is all just a game. We all agreed on the rules beforehand but for some magical reason we forgot about it. So we started taking it really seriously now and obviously, not remembering why we are doing it, we play as if our whole "life" depends on it! Or you can think about it as a film set. We all know our roles, so sometimes we have to act being cruel, but in reality it is not who we are. Or we play somebody who is really poor but we are paid millions for this role! What I really want to say is we already live in an abundant world. Just by changing our perception of the world, we start seeing a completely different picture. Accept things the way they are, be grateful for what you already have, focus on what you want to attract in your life, trust and believe in yourself and you will get there!

"Priorities lead to prosperity."

How important is money to you? What is it that you want it for? Is there anything more important to you? Maybe it is your family or values like intelligence and you have a wrong belief, probably a belief of your parents that intelligent people can't be rich? I knew somebody a long time ago who had a PhD in psychology and who tried to make money so hard but never succeeded. First, he strongly believed that only fools get lucky and become rich and intelligent people (like him) have to work really hard to just make a living. (What an unfair world!) Secondly, he hated all rich people. He, at one point, had three jobs and investments and still only had enough money to just pay the bills. He was also very jealous of his parents who were very well off and thought it was unfair they didn't help him as much as they could. His situation only got worse as his wife started seeing another man for money! He is still struggling and things won't change for him if he doesn't change his attitude about money and wealth.

The lesson is, it is not how hard you try, if you are blocking yourself from prosperity, you are the only one who can open the door and let the wealth come into your house! Make it important to you, really important. Start reading financial articles, get educated or get people around you who are already wealthy so you can learn from them. Get rid of negative beliefs, start thinking of what you would really love doing in your life, because it is possible to do what you love doing and get paid for that! Actually it is the only way it should be.

I remember when I was a little girl it made me really sad to see all those people around me who worked such long hours every day and earned very little. I started earning some pocket money when I was 13. My sister and I used to help our grandma to sell berries and fruit in the market. We looked at people who had been doing that for years and were so unhappy in their lives. We decided we would only do what we enjoyed doing and made fun out of it. It was still a very early start, a long day on our feet, heavy baskets, but we looked on it as a game and enjoyed that. A few years later I started giving private English lessons to school children, and that was a more rewarding and interesting job.

I always knew that to do a quality job you need to enjoy it, so everything I do in my life I try only seeing positive sides of things and now I don't even know – is it I am doing what I love, or loving what I do? You might say, it is being adaptable, yes, at some point it is, but it is not being content – I am always looking for new possibilities and setting new goals! It is just remembering that there is time for everything to happen and being grateful for where you are now.

Business plan.

You probably always thought that unless you intend to run a business, you don't need a business plan! In many people's perception a business plan is for raising money from potential investors only and therefore they never think about writing one. No, the business plan is for you, to know where you are going and how you are going to get there! Define your goals. What is it that you always wanted to do but "never had time" or "your family didn't allow you" or "because of your poor health" or "lack of knowledge" you decided would never work out? Make a list of all the things you would love to do in your life and then another list of what is really stopping you. Now imagine you are playing a game, in which you are in a role of a barrister and you have to find all the possible reasons to prove that it is still possible to do those things! If it is really hard for you to do it, call a friend and let him "be You" for this game and you have to provide all the arguments against the things that you wrote were stopping you.

Once you have done that and you know that you really can do things you love and get paid for that, start mapping out your plan to success. Write your main goals with a definite time frame and milestones to achieve those goals. Be as realistic as possible, though you might want to challenge and stretch yourself a bit! Then write a detailed plan of your every action, step by step. If you are not very good at planning and organising things – your first goal will be to become good at that.

Your wealth team.

We are all so different and we are good at certain things and not as good at others. Why? Because they are not as important to us. In this case, we don't need to try to become good at everything. That would be impossible! And so time consuming as well. Get the right people around you. You probably will do it anyway, unconsciously, without even thinking and planning it.

There was a time in my life when four of my friends left the circle of people I keep in contact with. They all left my life within a few months because I changed my vision. They were no longer in tune with my world perception and my plans. Those were people who were great companions to go out and "spend" time with. Time wasters like I was and it worked perfectly well for all of us! But then my vision changed. I didn't have time for them and they found me "different" and "boring" with all my new activities! This is fine; as we discussed earlier, people will come and go from our lives. Imagine you are in the market place, people all walk in different directions and you don't have to follow them all! This is life. Because if you need to buy oranges and somebody else is looking for cheese, you will not find them in one place! Therefore it is OK to stop and have a chat for a minute with somebody if you bump into each other, but now you don't have that obligation to go and help them look for cheese!

Our time is precious; we might not be given a second chance in this life, so spend it wisely. Find your team, more likely you will attract them into your life anyway. And maybe let some people go. We all change, evolve, grow, and we do it at a different pace. Accept the change and acknowledge that you are moving towards your goals.

The joy of living rich.

Imagine that, for whatever reason, money is no longer an issue in your life. Now you are free to pursue whatever you want to be, whatever you want to do or whatever you want to have. What would be on your list of things you want to change in your life? And what would you keep the same?

It is fascinating how little people would actually change their lives, if they had more money. Sure, they might buy a better car or a bigger house, take more holidays – but they wouldn't change their habits or leave their friends, stop eating in their favourite restaurants, watch different movies or laugh at different things.

In those areas of your life you wouldn't change, you are already leading a rich life! True and lasting happiness will never be a result of how much money you have got in your bank account, it is a product of living life with a meaning and purpose. That's why, to live a happy and fulfilling life, you don't need to wait until you have more money, you can start doing it right now!

Lastly, a small test to reveal how rich you are already.

What makes you the happiest in your life?

What makes your life meaningful and purposeful?

Who do you love and who makes you feel most loved?

What are your greatest pleasures in life?

What are you grateful for in your life?

How much would you sell your ability to see, hear, feel, smell, taste, love for?

How rich are you already?

1.5. Sexuality.

"If men and women act according to each other's liking, their love for each other will not be lessened even in one hundred years."

Kama Sutra

Men and women.

For thousands and thousands of years, men and women have felt attracted to each other, the result is the continuation of the human race. Though both genders have certain feelings, they never stop arguing and fighting. The reason is that we are different. It is only through understanding and accepting these differences that we can achieve harmony in our relationships.

Some people believe that sex tends to be more important to men, while romance is more important to women. With a deeper understanding of our sexual differences based on our genetic development and social role, we can start to understand each other better and stop being judgemental. Women sometimes overestimate the role of sex in men's lives and think they want only one thing – their bodies, while men think sex is not that important for women and we have sex sometimes to please men or withhold it to punish them.

The reason is, though we are both human beings, we are very different as genders. We look differently, we think differently and we behave in a different way! Men and women *do* think differently, at least where the anatomy of the brain is concerned, according to a new study.

The brain is made primarily of two different types of tissue, called grey matter and white matter. This new research reveals that men think more with their grey matter, and women think more with white. Researchers stressed that just because the two sexes think differently; this does not affect intellectual performance.

For a woman in order to connect, she needs to feel loved and cared for. For a man it is just the opposite – through sex he opens his heart and shows his love.

Sex is the chemistry of love and our most primal instinct. In Hindu thought, sex is not only considered natural and necessary but almost sacred, reflecting in human form the creation of the world.

Sex Is Our Body

The most obvious and most frequently talked about part of sex is the physical part that involves our bodies. The sexual parts of our bodies are usually considered to be the parts that relate to reproduction: the genitals. But every part of our body can play a role in sex. Learning more about how your body works when having sex, and how you can work it more, and better, can expand your definition of sex exponentially.

Sex Is Our Mind

It's often said that the greatest sex organ is the mind. How we think and feel about our bodies and ourselves, and how we interpret the physical contact we have with others is really what distinguishes good sex from bad. While some people worry about "over thinking" sex, the fact is that exploring our sexual thoughts and feelings may be much more important than trying the latest sex position or role-play outfit.

Sex Is Our Spirit

Sex and religion may appear to be unlikely bedfellows, but most major religions have a lot to say about sexuality. And besides, saying that sex can be defined in spiritual terms doesn't have to include organized religion. For some, sex is spiritual because they do feel like it brings them closer to a "higher power." For others it is their personal religious beliefs that guide their sexual behaviours. Regardless of how it impacts on you, your religious or spiritual beliefs and convictions make up part of your personal definition of sex, and exploring them is another way of exploring sex.

Sex is a reason for a great relationship and a means to it at the same time. When we feel happy with our partner we feel that we can show that to him or her while making love. On the other side, when we are having sex we feel closer to our partner.

Having great sex is not about improving our sex techniques.

While opening our minds to new experiences will help us to reach new heights in our sexual life, it is better communication and paying attention to the needs and desires of your lover that do the trick. Sexuality is not about having a perfect body and making all the right moves, it is about becoming one, feeling the rhythm and casting off inhibitions and merging into one energy flow. As in everything, the more you do it, the better you become. You learn to listen and understand. Your body learns to respond and get a different kind of pleasure.

Getting in the mood.

The essential part of lovemaking is seduction, the temptation of sensual desires. Taking your partner away from everyday concerns of life into a world of eroticism and sensuality will heighten their desire and the experience of sex will be even more intense and pleasurable. After a busy day it is important to focus on your partner, share your thoughts, maybe have a glass of wine. This will help you to unwind and synchronise with each other. Put on nice calming music, turn down the lighting. Tell each other how you feel and what you'd like to do. Surprising each other with gifts can add to your seduction. As well as greeting one another with flowers, chocolates, perfume or wine, you could be more obvious with lingerie or greet your partner naked at the door. Lightning candles and a log fire will make the setting even more romantic and the scent of essential oils and incense will help to stimulate your senses.

Taking a bath together is another wonderfully sensual and intimate way to begin lovemaking. Give your partner a relaxing and sensual massage. Involving all the senses before the actual sex will make your partner more exciting and the process more pleasurable. The Kama Sutra suggests many ways of stimulating the senses to heighten well being and increase sexual appetite, from entertaining your lover with music to feeding them aphrodisiac foods or adorning them with flowers. You probably know what your partner loves. If you don't know and you are too shy to ask, you can suggest some things and watch your partner's reaction. Sometimes we don't know what we like because it might feel different with another partner.

Sexuality is all about connection. Once you are on the same wavelength you know exactly what your partner wants from you, you finish their words and fulfil their desires before they actually asked anything. Be open to new experiences and don't be afraid of talking about your desires. Good communication is the key to great sex, but sometimes you don't need words. It is the chemistry that connects you and it is so powerful that it seems, without any effort, you are having the most amazing sex ever. Unfortunately no book in the world will teach you how to connect and have great sex. It is something you have to discover yourself through years of practice.

1.6. Spirituality.

"We are born into the world of nature; our second birth is into the world of spirit,"

Bhagavad Gita

Religious via spiritual.

Our life is a long journey of discovery. We learn new things from the day we are born. First we are taught by our parents, later we have teachers, mentors, friends, television and books. Our whole life we are surrounded by tons of information. We are taught to believe in what we see, what we can understand and explain with our rational minds. But there are some things we can only learn ourselves, through believing and then through knowing, tapping into the power of our minds, going well beyond logic, into the realm of spirituality.

You are likely to have received some minimal spiritual training through your religion. However, this is a level below, we are looking at truth through different sets of glasses and each of them interprets the truth in its unique way. The wonderful gift of religion is the teaching that we are all spiritual in nature; the biggest drawback is that it teaches us that we should obey rules and regulations, putting boundaries on our limitless souls.

There are no boundaries in this universe and by limiting ourselves with religion we limit our potential.

Saying that Christianity is right and Judaism is wrong is like saying France is a fake and Britain is real. It is still the same world; it is about where you put your boundaries. Just imagine how much you would miss out if you believed England is the only country to be in. Accepting that you are a part of the world opens you thousands of doors and millions of exciting opportunities.

These kinds of things you most likely don't learn at school, so you might have adopted a sceptical attitude toward the spiritual, imagining someone being spiritual in constant prayer and meditation. Everybody has different ways of tapping into the knowledge of the universe. And to connect to the higher self you only need yourself and a clear mind, be open to receive what you ask for. Whether you look for it or not it is still out there, waiting to be discovered by you.

Purpose in life.

Our greatest gift from God is our life. Your answer to it is what you can give back. Finding the purpose and living it is our greatest task in life. We are born with a purpose and we have a lifetime to discover it. On the path of your journey you will stumble over some rocks thinking, "why me?" After a while when you recover you will be able to look back and see why that happened. So now you have a choice – you can continue suffering and blaming circumstances or you might learn and believe there is a reason for it, and whatever occurs it is for the better. You will learn to see the positive side of things and use your personal experience in most beneficial way. You will see obstacles as opportunities and will start looking for challenges. It can be a very entertaining trip full of surprises and excitement. This path is for focused and goal-orientated people, who know what they want. A path for adventurers and achievers.

There is a third way though. It is a very small path going across the high mountains of life. Very few people take it – it looks like a lonely path and full of difficulties so many people choose other roads. That is the path where miracles happen. This is the shortest path to the top, where you are walking in rhythm with time, the path where things come to you instead of you looking for them everywhere, the path where the news being delivered, the path where the wind brings you freshness and revelation even if you still cannot see beyond the horizon, the path of certainty and wisdom, the path of consciousness, of having a task in life.

Everything in the universe has a purpose. The invisible flow of intelligence which goes through everything in a purposeful way, including you. Try to view your life now through a different perspective. Look beyond your rational mind, see invisible things and listen to silence. Ask for it and it will come to you when you are ready.

Harmony.

When you know that you have purpose in your life, you experience total harmony, which comes from not having to strive for anything else. You experience life in a new, wholesome way. This is where you realise – it is all about seeing the big picture, your purpose and paying attention to the smallest details. Have you ever felt total comfort, like time stopped and all the sounds, colours, smells around you intensify hundreds of times? I experience it a lot. I walk down small streets in Holland Park and suddenly realise how beautiful the world is. These moments of love and joy make up our lives –whether it is a connection with loved ones or nature and enjoying solitude, contemplating and reflecting on life. You feel that you are being watched over and your actions come from inner beauty and harmony.

Cause versus Effect.

Which side of equation are you on? Cause or effect? Taking responsibility for your actions is not easy, and sometimes we want to say that we are not leaders and we are happy to follow somebody else. Certainly we are all different and some have to be leaders and others are here to implement ideas - that is the synergy of interdependence and integrity.

According to Napoleon Hill, these are the major attributes to Leadership:

- Unwavering courage
- Self-control
- A keen sense of justice
- Definiteness of decision
- Definiteness of plans

- The habit of doing more than you get paid for
- A pleasing personality
- Sympathy and understanding
- Mastery of detail
- Willingness to assume full responsibility
- Cooperation.

To be a cause of your life you don't need to be a leader in life, but learning and acquiring some of their traits will definitely make you feel more grounded and in control. In this context, being spiritual means seeing the big picture and taking responsibility for everything happening, not just in your life but also in the world. That might sound ridiculous but in some way we are responsible for everything, even if it is a war on the other side of the world. Just as the state of your life is the reflection of your state of mind, so too is the state of the world a reflection of our collective state of mind. All that you see in the physical world has a mental equivalent in the minds of each of us. Understanding this leads to knowing that we are capable of creating a world we want to live in. Acknowledging this means you take responsibility and take control of your life.

Intuition.

There is no such thing on earth as coincidence. You might think that is a very blunt statement. How about "there is no luck"? Accepting those things would mean you take responsibility off your shoulders and give all the power to external circumstances. We attract luck and we make things look like amazing coincidences. Paying attention to invisible messages and knowing deep inside that there is something more than pure coincidence, is what you learn when living your purpose. Those little hunches inside you become stronger and clearer. Then you just know. You learn to ask yourself and get the answers whenever you need to. We call it intuition, gut feeling, something that "our heart tells us". Don't ignore it. Nurture it, cherish it and it will grow and bloom and reward you with wonderful miraculous power.

Some people view intuition as tapping into universal knowledge, some as God talking directly to them. I look at it as all of the above and as having a glance of the treasure inside us, getting to know ourselves better. I always pay attention when I feel something strongly inside me. My intuition tells me how to plan my days, when to write, what to buy, what to eat. You start trusting yourself and your body and mind responds to it by opening up. I rely on it in virtually all areas of my life. Every day I become more and more aware of it. I feel guided and immensely powerful. This is when miracles start happening in your life.

Miracles.

Deep inside you is a power of limitless possibilities, where all things are possible. Limits simply do not exist, and you seem always to be at the right place precisely at the right time. It is here where you can make synchronistic "unbelievable" connections with others and start almost reading other people's thoughts. It is here where you are able to meet precisely the right person to help you with a particular task or project you are working on. It is here where you suddenly hear a piece of news which makes the puzzle complete, it is here where you get the answer while you still haven't finished the question. This is the place where real magic takes place and begins to manifest in your physical world. This is the place of higher awareness, where mystery disappears and the purpose of your life becomes very clear to you.

When I say miracles I am not referring to turning rocks into gold or making things disappear like the illusionists on stage. When I speak about miracles I mean things you considered before beyond your capabilities to manifest in your life because of limiting beliefs you might have had. Getting your life to purpose and becoming more open and starting accepting things is the first step to becoming your own magician in life.

In my life I had to go through a sequence of steps in order to be at the point where I can be confident about what I write about and feel that my life is full of miraculous "coincidences". I am still walking on this path and I know it is going to be a long way full of amazing experiences and magic. We come across really unbelievable things in life and we think how lucky we are. I have a few stories like that but deep inside me I always knew it was a test, but never pure chance or luck. I like travelling. It is one of my passions in life. This is there I learn a lot of my lessons in life. Every time I go somewhere I kind of expect something to happen. I don't make my mistakes twice, but every time it is something completely new, some absolutely unpredictable thing.

I remember one of the first trips back home to Russia a few years ago. I was flying via Moscow where I had to change terminals and get my connection to Krasnodar where I have an apartment. I remember packing a few days prior to the trip and as my flight was in the late afternoon. As always I took my time and decided to go shopping for presents for my family. I came home 2-3 hours before my taxi was to arrive and then had that real sharp feeling inside me that I needed to check the flight time again. As it turned out my plane was to take off in an hour. I started panicking and literally shaking. I had never missed a plane in my life and my sense of logic turned off completely. I remember dialling for a taxi and explaining that I was very late but I still wanted to take the chance. I threw my passport and other papers into the bag and ran out into the street. The taxi arrived soon, but it was still at least half an hour, even if the traffic was good, to get to the airport. I jumped inside the car only to realise 5 minutes later I didn't have my mobile phone with me. It was too late to come back so we just carried on going. I rushed into the airport building half an hour before the plane took off, checked in, surprisingly they accepted my luggage and told me not to worry – I made it. I said hundreds of thanks to God, went through to the lounge and thought my adventure was over.

We arrived in Moscow on time and then I was supposed to take a shuttle bus that connects one terminal with another. It was about 90 minutes before the flight and I felt pretty confident. My luggage was the last piece on the conveyor and I managed to miss my bus. There was another coach in just 15 minutes. I didn't want to take a taxi as it was very expensive and I only had cash for the taxi in Krasnodar - as I told my dad not to meet me. He lives 85 km from the town and I would land at 4 am, so I wanted to make things easier for everybody. I took my coach, there wasn't much time left, so I started feeling a bit uneasy, especially when in 2 stops I realised that it was the wrong bus going to the centre of Moscow and now we were passing a wood on a lonely highway. I jumped out in the middle of nowhere, it was getting dark and I could see occasional lights of cars passing by. Strange, but at that moment I felt indifferent. I automatically raised my hand to stop a car, but they all had their own business in mind. In about 10 minutes a car stopped, a big jeep, and the man looked curious about what a young girl like me was doing on a highway with a suitcase at this time of the day. It was 30 minutes before my connecting flight. He asked me how much money I had. I had very little, but he agreed, even though he was going in a completely different direction. He took me through the forest, on a small road between trees. It was very dark by that time. Somehow I trusted him, did I have a choice? We got there with 10 minutes to spare, I gave him all the money I had and ran to the check in point. The girl saw that I was completely lost and asked for my passport. I realised I left my handbag with my passport at the security table. It was still there. She apologized and said they had closed the gate and all the seats were taken. Then she spoke to the manager and said they were upgrading me to business class and took my luggage. At this point I was just going with the flow. Logically I would be still in London. I smiled when I thought how I had called the travel company with the driver's phone on the way to Heathrow and asked them to hold the plane, because I was definitely coming.

I flew back to Krasnodar. It was early morning, but still pitch black outside. At the taxi rank I realised I didn't have any roubles and my phone was back in London. Somehow I negotiated with the taxi driver to take me home for some change in pounds and euros. (Amazing!) He agreed, I don't know why, but for some reason I knew he would. Still everything was closed and very silent. Getting close to my flat, I noticed some lights in the corner of the street. That was a 24 hours automatic machines shop open to insomniac customers.

I was tired and could only think of getting in bed in a few minutes time. I dragged my suitcase up the staircase trying to be as silent as possible. I think it was summer because my neighbour was sleeping outside on the terrace. Trying not to wake him up, I sneaked on tiptoes into the lounge and put the key in the door lock. It didn't fit. I tried again and again. No – it was definitely the wrong key. In desperation I woke up my neighbour and asked him for help. Nothing worked. And suddenly it occurred to me that last time I visited my flat was robbed and my sister changed the locks everywhere, but that was when I was already gone. The blood in my head was pulsating so strongly I could feel it. I ran down the road to the small game shop. There were no customers and the manager was very friendly. They heard my story, gave me some water, I was so dehydrated and let me use their phone to call my dad. That was still around 2.30 am and he had to drive for 2 hours to get to me. Then it was over. I think it was the longest day in my life.

Another time I was in Hamburg, flying back to London. We were celebrating the birthday of one of my best friends, Cat. It was an amazing party and then her parents came to take her to the seaside, while I went to the airport. Again, I had only cash for lunch, no credit cards and my phone credit was very low. I already had plans for that evening to see the guy I was dating at that time. We were together for more than a year, but it still wasn't a proper relationship and I never asked him about anything. As it happened they cancelled my flight back because I flew via Portugal and not directly from London. (I had booked two flights. I think it was either cheaper or easier.) Then they told me I didn't have a ticket any more. I didn't believe them. I thought it was some kind of mistake. So I talked to the manager and she confirmed that I had to buy a new ticket and they had only one ticket left in business class for 600 euros. I still thought it was negotiable. You know, when you have paid for the ticket, it is difficult to understand that it is no longer valid. It was still about two hours before the flight so I wasn't really worried. I thought somehow I would get on that plane! To cut a long story short, I did get on the plane. I bought the business class ticket with no money or credit card 5 minutes before the plane took off. And I had a wonderful date later.

The thing is if you really want something and focus on the solution, the whole universe conspires to help you. That was a miracle of its kind, and I didn't think I was just lucky. I trusted that higher intelligence and I knew it wouldn't let me down. Yes, I was nervous and panicking and running around and asking for phones from strange people and used my best skills of negotiation. But first of all I knew. And there was no other option for me that day. It is absolutely magical how powerful we are, with limitless possibilities, capable of achieving everything we put our mind to. Mostly we use it in extreme situations, because our logic and rational mind breaks down and let the higher unconscious power take the wheel. But we can use it in every day life and make fewer mistakes and live a truly magical life.

Spiritual beings with human experience.

"We are not human beings having a spiritual experience. We are spiritual beings having a human experience."

Teilhard de Chardin (French Geologist, Priest,

Philosopher and Mystic, 1881-1955)

Remember, everything begins with the thought. Here are some practical suggestions for getting in touch with yourself as a spiritual being.

- Write down all the things you experience beyond your five sensory system, note down all your intuitive hunches, keep a record for your own satisfaction;

- Practise strategic visioning. Imagine something you want to achieve in detail. Try to see the colours and hear the sounds around you. Make the picture really bright and real. Imagine yourself rising high above your time line and drop the picture on the line on the exact day you want it to happen. Remember your feelings;

- Spend some time by yourself reflecting on things, make no judgement of people and forgive them from your heart. Think of the things you are grateful about in your life.

- Remove the clutter from your house. Think about the place where you live, furniture, decorations. This is the reflection of your inner self. Unclutter your thoughts;

- Imagine yourself connected to everybody else in the world by a string. How does it make it feel knowing that we are all one?

- Try to keep your focus on purpose, not outcome.

Detach yourself from outcome. Believe deep inside whatever happens, it is for the best.

- Develop a loving and empowering attitude toward yourself. Get rid of any negative language. Restate the things you say focusing on positive. (Instead of saying I don't want to be fat - you can say I want to be fit and healthy.) Believe in your spiritual self. Ask and your questions will be answered.

1.7. Balance. Wholeness.

Set of mind/equilibrium.

Now, going back to the diagram at the beginning of the chapter - how round is your wheel? What is lacking in your life? What is perfect?

The good thing it doesn't have to be round all the time. We are not perfect, and we are constantly learning lessons. As long as you feel grounded and purposeful – and, ultimately, balanced – you are doing fine.

The right answers will come at the right time. Learn patience and the rest will come.

Sometimes when we feel a little bit unstable and want to fall and cry – the best thing would be to do exactly that. Pretending we are fine and continuing living and working in an old fashion will not help in this case. It is like our body saying to us - it is time to readjust and refill the tank. When we don't know the answers - the only thing we can do is to wait and just go with the flow. If at that minute we start craving for something - it could be the answer, but at the same time could be just short-term relief. Just keep in mind-at the end of the circle it is ok to be a bit down and rejuvenate. People around us always want to see us happy and smiling and it is great if we can be this way almost always! But it is absolutely fine to sulk from time to time and just let it go for a while.

For example, there are stressful moments in my life and at these moments I feel literally tired and not interested in things. My energy levels drop and I might lose my appetite or, on the contrary, start eating like mad. I learnt not to force myself to do things I would normally do, but just let my body decide what it wants to do – even if it is lying in bed the whole day!

When it is a nice sunny day I walk. Yes, just walk. Usually on these days I don't feel like exercising, so I just walk. Strolling for just one hour can do wonders for your mind and your body! You might want go for a swim or just stay in quietly with your favourite TV program. Anything would do if you feel comfortable doing it. When our body is sick - our doctors usually tell us to stay in bed and get as much rest as we can. But when our mind feels off balance nobody would prescribe us pills and tell us to stay in bed. But it is the same as being ill, only this time it is our mind cries for help!

Secret to your life.

Do the things that you love and that bring you joy. It is that simple. Smile. Laugh. Live as if it were your last day. Stop for a moment and look around. What would you do if you knew it was your last day on earth? (I don't mean writing a will and organising the funeral or killing all your enemies.) The thing is you would probably keep on doing the very same things you are doing now. Things that you love doing. Very simple things probably. Maybe there are two or three things you always wanted to do but didn't have enough courage? Or the right opportunity? So why not do it now? Say those words of love to somebody or make that phone call... Don't forget – if life is still a game – you are just exiting one of those games. So, what would you do differently today?

Test. How balanced are you?

Here is a test for you. Discover how balanced you are, where you achieve perfect equilibrium in your life and which areas you need to focus on. Don't think too much about every question, relax and let yourself give the answers. Enjoy!

1.   When did you worry last time?

•   Today

•   Within the last week

•   Within a month

•   Can't remember

---

2. When did you spend time doing your hobby?

---

3. How often do you go to the gym? (Do any kind of sport?)

---

4. If you look at what you ate in the last 24 hours, how healthy would you rate the food on the scale from 1- junk food to 10 - raw vegetables and fruit.

---

5. Do you find yourself attractive?

---

6. Are you in love?

---

7. Are you in the kind of relationship you want to be?

---

8. If you have a partner, take a few minutes and calculate his/her total score on the magic wheel. For each branch you give maximum 10 points

---

9. Do the same for yourself.

---

10. Are you studying anything at the moment? (This can be any subject – from cooking or gardening to taking a course in karate.)

---

11. Do you feel emotionally strong? How strong on a scale from 1 to 10?

---

12. To feel comfortable, how much more (less) should your income be? (Multiply by how much.)

---

13. Do you think you are good at money management?

14. Do you think you are greedy? (Emotionally attached to money?)

15. Do you think you are sexy?

16. Do you get lots of attention from the opposite sex?

17. Do you feel young? (Just by the way you look? Behave?)

18. What age do other people think you might be? (Ask three people who don't know how old you really are.)

19. If you could compare your life to one of the following, which would it be?

- Theatre (You always play different roles and adapt.)

- Game (Fun? We are all either winners or losers? You can always have another go.)

- Jungle (Fight, competition.)

- Jail (Boredom and purposeless.)

- Your own definition.

20. Do you trust your intuition?

_____

21. How happy do you feel? (On a scale from 1 to 10?)

_____

I am not going to judge you by the answers. This is just for you to get a picture of your current life. Are you happy with your answers? Is there something surprising in them? How do you want your life to be from now on?

Section 2:
The Seven Principles of Life.

We are born. Then we feel loved and cared about. We explore this new world and learn new things, absorbing everything like a sponge. We take. It is natural to us. We learn to share. We grow older and learn many more things. We may freeze at some level and stop learning anything new. At this moment we start growing old. Another scenario - we keep on learning. We take responsibility and take charge. We are in charge of our life, our fate. We start seeing the big picture. At this moment we learn acceptance and patience. We give our love back into the world and fill our hearts with gratitude. We get a priceless experience. We find harmony, become complete and immerse ourselves in eternity.

2.1. Childish Curiosity.

From our very first breath our whole life depends on how curious we are and eager to learn. The faster we learn – the better our chances to adapt in this world.

A piece of new information can literally change our life. How do we know which is right for us to take on board and what is not? Every second we are bombarded with two million pieces of information. Our brain isn't able to process such a huge amount of data, so all information goes through our incredibly designed system - special filters, such as our beliefs, attitudes, focus and at the end we are left only with 4 to 7 bits which we are able to process. We only see what we focus on. Try this exercise for a minute. Look around yourself and count all the objects in red. Remember the shape, their position, are they still or moving? Done? Now close your eyes and.... ask yourself how many yellow objects did you see? Most likely you noticed none! And that is what we are doing on a daily basis – we program our brain to look for specific information and that is what we see. Two different people go onto the streets of London and do you think they see the same things? Absolutely not. A postman on the corner of the street will see something different from what you or I will see. Do you think we see the same opportunities? No, but it doesn't matter, because we have different goals set and different purposes to fulfil. At any moment we can change our program and start seeing new things immediately!

Sometimes we don't realise why we are looking at particular things at the moment and then one day the mosaic comes together and we see the Big Picture.

When I came to London, for the first few years I tried a few different things, which all led me to where I am now. A few years ago, after being really into fashion design and planning to set up my fashion label, I suddenly turned around 180 degrees and went into finance. Why? I don't know exactly. There were a few issues, first - I needed a work permit to be able to run a company and second - I ran out of capital. I was reading everything I could find in the market, subscribed to financial periodicals and started visiting meetings for traders and investors. Very soon I actually tried my hand in the market. I went through success and failure, but still didn't see it as a main destination. I enjoyed that, but somehow knew I was being prepared for something different.

Then, as unexpectedly as before, I dipped into the world of psychology and self-help. I was devouring hundreds of books on NLP, hypnosis and other similar subjects; went to a few different seminars and workshops. I thought – this is it! This is exactly what I want to do and trading was just something that led me to where I am now. I met a few interesting people and we started working on a few projects. That's where the idea to write a book was born. We had a few disagreements and carried on in different directions. All this time I considered myself highly unemployable and thought that I could only lead a company and be my own boss. My number one value was freedom and I thought I was in a perfect place. I was. But it wasn't a destination, only a start. Putting freedom first cost me dearly. Not only I wasn't able to commit in relationships but because of my own limitations I had to go through the process of "bending the fences". The Universe wanted to convince me it was all just in my mind. So suddenly I met a man, with him I realised freedom is not everything and landed a job in a city in a very fast expanding brokerage company where I was thrown straight into sales. There I realised why I had studied markets and psychology. They wove together perfectly and still gave me that sense of flexibility and though attached to one place – the sense of being my own boss (we work on commission) I don't think I am at the final place any more. Now I know that the way is going to be long and interesting, full of new exciting things so I can never miss a new opportunity to learn.

Another thing I noticed – whatever you do, you should look at things from the perspective of learning. Maybe this very low paid job will lead you to an amazing job you always dreamed about. Well, here I can't help – you should feel it with your heart. Sometimes the whole event happens, so you could meet that contact who will introduce you to somebody else and after a chain of events you will come to realise that you achieved what you originally planned, but maybe in a way you never expected you would!

Learning can be used in different contexts as well. Get to know those around you. Pay attention to the smallest detail, impress your loved ones. People love that. Make those around you feel important. That is one of our primal needs (look at the pyramid of Maslow). People will remember you for that. Of course we can't remember everything and anything! It is impossible. But again, we don't need to. I call them remembering "only important things". What is important for you? Sometimes giving a call to somebody you haven't seen for a while on their birthday can make their day! This works, believe me. Start from small things, be attentive to your colleague or ask somebody how they feel after that cold they caught last Friday. You will be surprised the effect these small things can have. Why do you think you are paying that money for the first class airplane ticket? If it was just food it would cost maybe an extra hundred pounds, but not ten times more. It is all about getting that extra attention and care, those small details.

Go on, become inquisitive, attentive and open to new things! Make your life more inspiring and exciting. You will be surprised how much more fun it will be. Don't be afraid of trying new things. At least you will have new stories to tell. All I am saying is - we only have that long life and a few good chances. Yes, we are making things happen, but sometimes we have to fall ten times before we learn to walk. There is no shortcut and we all have to go through that. But if we don't try we will never get! Do something new today. Before arguing, just assume for a second it can be right, at least for somebody else. Become more flexible and adaptable. Your life might take a new exciting course before you ever notice! At one point you realise why it happened to you and that's where you will see the big picture.

2.2. Seeing a Big Picture.

I don't have the answers to all questions- but I believe you do. The moment you start seeing beyond the horizon, your life finds purpose. What purpose it is – I don't know. I have my own purpose and I believe it is something that can evolve through our whole life. But seeing the big picture is knowledge. Knowing where you are going. Some people call it intuition. It can be very subtle or very intense. There are no rules in this case. From the moment you decide you are going to trust yourself, this invisible force will guide you to your destination. You might not recognise it straight away. Sometimes it can even feel very annoying, not understanding why these particular things happen to you.

I remember we went skiing in Courchevel with a friend of mine. It was our last day and we didn't expect the weather to be nice, but then the sun came out and we decided to have a last go. We rushed to the lifts, walked up the stairs leading to the bubbles and waited in a queue for some time. I remember it was swelteringly hot and we were carrying our skis.

People encouraged by the lovely weather kept on coming. It was our turn to go through the gates and then we realised our cards were not working! I remember being very upset and angry and all we could do was go all the way down. Certainly we could call the hotel and they would arrange new cards for us in less than fifteen minutes. By that time everybody woke up and flooded the lift entrance. We lost probably more than forty minutes, but still were very excited when we eventually got through. At the very moment we jumped off our lift seats we noticed a man changing a notice board for a piste that was closed before. As it was heavily snowing the day before all the territory was covered with a thick layer of snow and they had to close a few routes because of the avalanche risk. We looked around and we realised that we were the first people going to ski down this route, freshly covered with snow. All I remember is it was just unbelievable! It was so much fun to ski down and leave our marks on the snow. To fall down on purpose and play with the snow and throw snowballs at each other. It felt like getting a big present right at the end of our trip! In less than an hour the wind started blowing and it started snowing heavily again so we had to ski back to the resort. But I will always remember those moments as one of the most amazing times in my life.

Later that evening we were discussing the day, we were still very excited about the morning's luck, and then my friend said that if it wasn't for our cards not working at the beginning, we would have missed the whole experience and would have just continued skiing in a different direction.

It struck me that these things happen to us all the time. We miss a bus and then meet somebody who makes a difference in our life. Or we give somebody a chance and it turns out to be the biggest decision of our lives, just months later. We all have our own stories. The lesson is not to anticipate things to be perfect all the time but allow ourselves to be given these presents of fate from time to time. Believe that things happen for a reason and eventually we will understand that, but at the moment it might not be visible for us.

There are certain characteristics which mark out people who are able to see the Big Picture. The first one is being fearless and adventurous. As you know - if you don't try - you don't get. The people who jump at opportunities that come in their way, know that at some point this event might bring them to their goal. The second virtue is patience. Most things don't happen overnight and need some time and preparation. Number three feature is trust. If you trust and believe in yourself then everything is achievable. Your brain is a super powerful computer and transmitter of information which is not available for our other senses to read and it is attuned and programmed to achieve your goals, so it filters out everything not relevant. And this is your fourth and probably most important tool-being focused. All the rest will follow.

Remember the film 'Pay Check' with Ben Affleck where Michael Jennings (Ben Affleck) is a highly intelligent electronics engineer who works on lucrative contracts for companies on secret projects. So secret that his paymasters are obliged to selectively erase his memory – from the time he starts working on a project to the time it ends.

His second project, which is pretty much the subject of the movie, is of a truly extraordinary nature. It is a time machine that its owners want to sell to governments at great profit.

This element makes the movie intellectual, and director John Woo deserves much credit for bringing out the story in this way. Before Michael gets into his second project, he meets Rachel at a party. Rachel is a biologist who works at the company that wants to build this ultimate machine. Michael and Rachel have a short but interesting conversation by way of mutual introduction.

Well, the second project is of three years' duration, and it presumably happens, but we don't actually see Michael working on it. Instead the movie fast-forwards to three years later. There is this time machine. Michael built it. He can see into his future and the future of the world. He sees terrible things and wants to prevent them from happening, effectively changing the future.

The problem is - his memory of the project will be erased on its completion. How then will he prevent the awful future? Here is how.

Michael, having travelled into the future, has pictures and newspaper headlines of the horrific things that happen when governments are allowed unfettered use of the time machine. Knowing that he will have no recollection of any of this, the future Michael sends present Michael clues of this black future through various innocuous means so that present Michael may try to alter the course of events.

Imagine now that this is happening in our lives on a daily basis. You might not believe in it and think it is all "coincidences" and "luck", but just imagine that some power of which we are a part, has planned our whole trip. Of course with some amendments, but with a certain destination. And maybe these events happening to us are just clues that inside us we definitely know where we are going and why. But in this game called life our memory was erased for some bigger purpose.

2.3. Taking Responsibility.

The day we decide that we are the cause, not an effect, we take responsibility for our life. It is intriguing and exciting. We are kings in our small kingdoms, and things are going to be exactly as we decide them to be.

How would that feel to know that you are always in control? Even when it seems as if everything goes against you, you still know that you are on the right track. I know it might sound very contradictory, but in our perfect world everything is perfect, therefore, everything is right.

It is much easier to say that "things happen to you" and that "it wasn't my fault" and keep on blaming people and circumstances around you. It is much harder is to become a true leader –somebody who not just organises people but takes responsibility for their actions.

You can start practising with small things. Next time something "happens to you", think of 10 reasons how you could cause it to happen. Be creative. When we know we caused it in some way, we feel much better that if we knew somebody else made it happen.

In many cases it is not very obvious, to say the least. When people starve on the other side of the planet we don't feel we caused it. Here is a big difference - feeling responsible and feeling guilty. There is no reason for us to feel guilty ever, because you can always find an explanation.

Even if you hurt another person, it could be that you

didn't wish this to happen, and it is not a coincidence things turned around this way. If you knew what you were doing and realised it wouldn't be possible not to upset somebody with your actions but still did, you still can feel responsible but not guilty. Perhaps you don't share the same values with that person or the time came when he or she had to leave your life. Or maybe, if you believe in reincarnation, you owed that to the person from your last life. There is an explanation for everything.

Once upon a time there lived a Little Soul. She was playing all day long and felt very happy. One day Little Soul felt really fed up with doing nothing. She went to her old friend, Big Soul and said: "I want to do something different, I want to go down to Earth and learn something new!" And Big Soul says; "What is it that you want to learn, my friend?" The Little Soul thought for a while and said: "I want…I want to learn Forgiveness!" "Forgiveness? And how are you going to do that?" "I know," Little Soul replied, "Let's go down to Earth together and live like human beings. And then you do something really horrible to me, so I can forgive you!" And the Big Soul said: "That's a great idea! Sure, let's do it, but, please, promise me now, when I do that terrible, horrible thing to you, you will remember that I only do it, because I dearly love you and want to help you."

We might not know it, but it is again about trusting yourself and the Universe and allowing yourself to take some guidance and lessons. You probably heard the saying that a butterfly can cause a hurricane on the other side of the planet with a move of its wing, if the conditions are right. You know from your experience that with a "right" word you can change your life, lose or win the competition, make a friend or an enemy, become famous or lose your reputation forever. Small things matter. Sometimes they are so small we don't realise the impact they might have.

So which part of the equation are you on? Cause or effect? In charge or a victim of circumstances? We often say that we didn't want it to happen. But did we really? Maybe we made ourselves "available" for that event to happen. Fear is the main reason people abdicate their responsibility. But it is by practising courage that we become courageous, like any other skill it can be acquired. If you can't play the piano, it would be stupid to say that it is your parents' fault they never took you to a music school. For things you really love and want – you always manage to find time and money.

Take on board everything you learnt so far and think of different situations when you thought you were really unlucky or when you were really upset with somebody. Is there any chance you could be responsible for that happening? Maybe indirectly somehow? Is there any chance that you can think of a possibility that you caused it? If you still think it was absolutely nothing to do with you, think about yourself as a part of the Universe. We all connect on an energy level and dimensions like time and matter are all very relative. With our five senses only we are like blind and deaf people in the middle of the busiest roads of Moscow – this can be compared to our ability to read the Universe language. And in terms of time span, our life is seconds to the existence of the Universe. Why do we have to go through this process? Again and again? Maybe to learn the lessons and make fewer mistakes in the future. Maybe the whole process was designed for a particular reason? This question will never be answered, because as soon as we know the answer we cease to exist. I am not here to answer this question. But I know that with our thoughts we change the planet. We change it every day. And the quality of our questions determines the quality of our life. And I take responsibility for everything happening in my life, because I am the cause. I create my own circumstances and I know we all can.

2.4. Accepting and Sharing.

Learning to accept is the greatest gift on its own. Accepting can be synonymous to the biggest virtue – patience. It comes to us from seeing the Big Picture.

It is OK for things to happen. Things happen all the time and with everybody. Although we are all unique, we all share the same ability to accept things the way they are. Not many of us do. Some just complain, some fight their way through, some, who consider themselves more sophisticated, ignore things.

What do you do when things are not the way you wanted them to be or expected them to be? Learning to take things the way they are is the greatest virtue you can have. You acquire the power to overcome all life challenges, have the most incredible life doing things you love doing and getting wherever you planned to get.

People talk a lot about philanthropy nowadays. Giving and sharing is great, though it depends if it is truly from your heart or you did it just for tax purposes or another self-interested reason. We start learning to give from an early age, when we have to share toys with our brothers and sisters. So from our early years we learn that giving is good, at which point taking is not considered so good. "If somebody offers you a sweet/drink/present you should politely say no." When we grow up, accepting can become even harder. Usually we don't even ask for things. Of course not all of us, but it is quite common, because that is the way well brought up/well mannered people are supposed to behave.

Accepting is multi-dimensional. First we must learn to accept all good things coming to us - whether it is a gift from a friend or invitation to an around the world trip in a private jet from a stranger. Well, it might happen as well, but then it is you who will have to cope with the consequences. I believe we are all quite good at accepting non-material things, like our close ones' time, actually we usually take it for granted. This is one of the more difficult things to come to accept. It is lowering our bar at expectations to the point where we are happy with what we have. So nothing can really upset us anymore. If we get something – we get excited and genuinely happy. If we lose – we accept the situation and appreciate things even more.

Accepting life the way it is with all its challenges and obstacles is a challenge on its own. But you will get there. If you already see the Big Picture you won't have any problems accepting things, because it is a part of the package.

What if a disaster doesn't happen to you but to somebody you really love or to those "innocent people caught up in the tsunami"? It is a part of the process and though we are all interconnected they have their own purposes in plans in life. They have their lessons and we should respect that. I know it might sound ridiculous, accepting that somebody dies from hunger – not if we can help it, we are still humans and we should collaborate in situations like that. But if we can't do anything about it, there is no need to feel guilty and punish ourselves. Our planet changes all the time – some species become extinct and trying to save them goes against Universe sense! Even stars die at some point. Our planet evolves all the time; if dinosaurs didn't die out millions of years ago, human beings would never have been born. It is a never-ending circle and we should accept that. We all die eventually anyway, but in any case we will never leave unless we accomplished the mission we came with, whether it is a ninety-year-long task or just a few minutes mission.

So why should we learn to take and accumulate tangible and intangible things through our whole life? All that would be pointless if we didn't give it away. But sharing always comes after taking, otherwise it wouldn't be possible! Remember in the aeroplane, the emergency instructions: "Put the safety mask first on yourself and only then on your child". I believe sharing gives you the greatest pleasure: knowing you were able to achieve the position where you can give and make somebody else a little bit happier. Even if it is a smile or a few minutes of your time – it might cost nothing to you – but will maybe make another person's day.

When an opportunity arises I try to show those small gestures of love whenever I can. It makes me happy as well. Some people believe you can never get anything for nothing. Which is to some extent true, but it is a more complicated issue to discuss in a small book like this. They might see your generosity as pure luck and even if they are wrong, because believe me or not, they deserved it, they might change their whole view on a subject and therefore change their life in the long term.

Imagine giving flowers to a strange woman in the street. Maybe you think she is pretty, maybe she reminds you of somebody else or maybe you just had those flowers in your hands and as they no longer serve the previous purpose (your girlfriend just dumped you over the phone) you can just give them to somebody else. And maybe that "lucky" girl had a negative belief about men for ages –she thought they were unromantic, selfish and not caring because of some man she met a long time ago. And by accepting those flowers she might regain her confidence in herself and get curious about men again. You never know. But these things happen all the time. Next time you have an opportunity to share something, even if is just good news, don't hesitate. You may really surprise somebody.

Always remember – the greatest gift you can ever share is knowledge and love. All material things cease to exist. Knowledge can transform people's lives and love can make them happy. There is a saying - instead of giving a man a fish a day, teach him to how to fish. Sharing doesn't have to be unconditional only. In order to give we need to be able to produce first. Life is amazingly just and it gives us all the tools we need to create our perfect world. And if it asks something in return, we should be glad to give it.

2.5. Gratitude.

London is a great place to learn gratitude. Every time we have a glimpse of sunshine – we feel grateful. We appreciate and value things we wish we had more. The biggest challenge is to learn to be grateful for things we have in abundance. Usually it is a sudden loss of these that makes us realise how important they were.

For example, being grateful for living in the 21st century, not fifty years earlier, because, "it was a better time, everything was cheaper, people were smarter, the planet was more beautiful and less polluted and nowadays is so tough." Not in fifty years' time. But Now. Think about it for a moment. Whatever happened in the past – it is an experience now. Future – we don't know about it. And we still are able to design it and change things. But we have the greatest opportunity to enjoy every moment of Now. So let's make the most of it.

Some people live in their past – constantly analyzing their "mistakes" or living on good memories. Some people live in the future - "when I get that qualification, when I meet a decent man, when I save that money." So they postpone their life and never actually enjoy it to the full. Those are all lousy excuses. We can never be 100% sure what is going to happen next. Actually the Universe likes to surprise us from time to time, especially when we are most confident about life. Sometimes life likes to play with us, why don't we play with it in return and enjoy every moment of the game?

How much are you enjoying your life now? Are you happy? When was the last time you laughed from the bottom of your heart? When did you feel really grateful towards somebody or something? Whatever your situation at the moment, you can change it. You have the most powerful tools on earth to do so. What do you do when you want something from a person? Probably you behave in a good manner toward him or her. Perhaps you even make an extra effort. The same is happening in the Universe. We always have big demands from it, but do we ever say thank you? Look around yourself. See the beauty in the world around you, in the sunshine, in the sound of falling rain, in the uniqueness of a flower or people's faces. There is perfection in everything. But it may be hidden from human sight. Look for it, appreciate it, and enjoy it.

We are energy and our thoughts are streams of condensed energy with a certain vibration frequency. When we are grateful we exude energy of a very high frequency, which in turn attracts the same quality of energy in return. Therefore we attract amazing things in our life. It can be easy to be grateful for the gifts our life surprises us with, being grateful for lessons we get in life can be a much more difficult task. But it is something we can all learn. Only by experiencing things can we learn how to deal with them in the future. Or maybe this "unlucky" event will lead us to something incredible.

If you already feel you can see a Big Picture, take control of your life and accept life the way it is, learning to be grateful won't be hard for you, it is probably already with you and you live a happy fulfilling life and enjoy challenges. If it is something you never thought about before – this is the best time to take it on board. Do something really enjoyable today, even if it is something you do every day. Realise how lucky you are to be able to do it! Life is only as beautiful as we are ready to see it.

2.6. Love.

The Universe is based on Love. It is that divine energy which keeps the planet alive and makes things happen. Just think how powerful this energy is. People do crazy things for the sake of love. Nothing like love opens your eyes and makes you see things in a different light. We sometimes say love "blinds" us. Another way to say that is it takes us to a different dimension, to the place invisible to other people.

Most people experience love. Some only love once, some fall in love dozens of times. What is love? Is it some kind of energy that makes you strong and weak at the same time? Energy that takes away common sense and opens your heart to new feelings? Energy that cures and makes you suffer the most?

I see love as an endless blue ocean which is never changing but never the same. One day it is calm and has a glass surface and seems to be merging with the horizon. Its purity and stillness somehow reassures you, fills your heart with certainty and strength. Another day it looks playful and bright and catches sparkly reflections from the sun and you are full of energy and enthusiasm. And then it rebels and roars and millions of tiny drops spray into the air and you become frightened, unsure and jealous. Next minute it comes down and fills you with serenity and peacefulness. It is never right or wrong. It is just beautiful. It is Love.

One day maybe we learn how to control our feelings. Not to restrict it or avoid it but immerse ourselves in it and make it sing for us. It is like playing the violin. It could be very hard and tedious work to learn to play it, but when you listen to its magnificent sound you think the musician is a genius – the skill seems so unreachable.

Once you have decided you are ready – it will come to you. But love is not a cherry cake. It is an ever-evolving entity with lessons and new experiences. It is the kind of energy that has the power to change in the shortest periods of time - nearly instantly - and people never realise –that it was them who made a decision. Learning should be a joyful experience and love is something that can teach us a lot. We all have those love stories. When we look back we realise that was a great experience and we are glad we moved on. It is never bad. It is just that change scares us sometimes.

Love is what makes our heart beat. We live in a relative world we compare things based on our experience. Love is absolute. It is what makes the sun shine, it is everywhere and it is constant and eternal. It makes everything possible. It is Light.

When you are in love, you know it is the most beautiful thing that ever happened to you. You don't want it to go. Sometimes it possesses us to the point that it poisons our life. So why is love given to us? Is it just for the purpose that we create a family and continue our generation? I believe it is also our strongest tool of change. It is what shakes us the most and pushes us to make decisions we never thought to be possible before. But you always allow it in your heart. You always make yourself available first. It never comes without permission. If it is not appropriate for a moment it becomes like a drug. One day you realize you are addicted and you are not happy any more. You feel like you can't live without it. But you can. You learn your lesson and move on. You might still have a trace left. It can be big and visible like a scar or can be a pleasant memory in a few years time. Again, it is you who chooses - always.

Love never disappears completely from our lives. It can take another form – but it is always here. It is a source of life. It gives life and takes it.

We all feel the need to love. And when we are in love for the first time – we all know – it is a unique incomparable feeling. We all want to be loved as well, because if it is one-way love, it is not complete. Nothing is a substitute for it. With love we see colours in the world, and what our life was before now seems to be a never-ending grey morning.

There are different kinds of love – love for our parents, which is similar to gratitude in a way, love for our friends, love for our second half, which is the strongest and the most mysterious one, love for people in general. There are more complicated forms of love, like love for our enemies or people who think differently. It all has the same base though. There is also another sort of love - the one when we don't need anything back, unconditional love, and that's the most powerful energy in the world. It is like lighting hundreds of candles with just one - making the world brighter and warmer. It is very different kind of energy because it brings results of another dimension. We are not immediately satisfied and we are not expected to be. But it all comes back to us multiplied many times. It is the purest kind of energy and it never vanishes forever. Love is stronger than hate. Hate and anger are similar feelings and they are all created in our minds. Love can dissolve any conflict and make the world a better place to be.

We all have oceans of love and they need to be constantly shared; it is like mixing it with oxygen to keep it alive. Light the world around you. Share your love and help to spread it around the world and fill people's hearts with eternal light. It is a journey of a lifetime but it is worth every day of it.

2.7. Growth and readjustment.

The mastery of life is the art and science of how to keep all your life's components in perfect balance. And it is not easy because we grow and evolve all the time.

We always readjust. Like a mechanical clock we need a little bit of rewinding from time to time. Whatever happens to us, however hard the knock was, we always stand up. With time passing by we adapt to new circumstances and consider it a norm. The quicker you are able to do that, the better your chances to achieve more in life. There is no right or wrong in here, it is just that for some people it is easier to move on faster, some need to stay longer in a swamp and reflect on life.

Imagine you are an underground train driver. You do your shifts – days and nights. (Somehow you think you are irreplaceable and the only person who can cope with it.) You feel you are responsible for carrying people around the city. Every day is the same route. The same routine. You like your job. You know your way well. It is your way of life now and you never stop. Have you ever felt that way? First you think – this is my world. As years go by you start thinking that – that is the world. You get used to the darkness of tunnels and lights at the end. To the wheel and the timetable in front of you. That's all you need. You feel content, life is never changing.

At this point you forget why you came here at the very beginning. You can forget, but the Universe can't.

You have two choices: either you carry on for a while and if you don't get back to the track you will have to leave and come back again in a different form in order to accomplish your mission. Another option - something unexpected happens to give you leverage to wake up and move on.

So maybe your train goes off the rails one day and you will have to go out to find help. You will get out of the tunnel up in the busy street and maybe you see sunshine for the first time in many years or the sound of outside buzz will touch something inside you and it will come to you – this is life! Or maybe you see it all and realise how much you love your job, but maybe you should come out more often. We get this kind of help all the time. We want to do more with our lives, to grow, to enjoy things, to bring change into the world.

Stagnation is never good. Sometimes it can be useful to slow down a bit and think – maybe it is time to change direction or go the opposite way? When we stop evolving - we grow old and die. So when opportunity comes to you and you decide to take it knowing it might change your life completely, don't rush with your decision. Think, are there enough good reasons to stay in the life situation you are now? If you find enough evidence to convince you to stick to the old way then stay longer. If your heart tells you the opposite - don't hesitate and make the jump. There are only two ways in this situation. It is like crossing the bridge. You can be only on either side of the river. But how long can you stay in the middle of the bridge? You might stay long enough to get used to it. Some people do. Or you may become so miserable and unsure that the only way out you can see is jumping in the river.

The truth is, we have to cross those bridges all the time in our lives. And though it can be a bit uncertain (what is there on the other side?) it is nothing to be afraid of. Remember, it is a part of our adventure to find that treasure.

Section 3:
Putting it all in Practice.

3.1. Designing your destiny.

"Would you tell me, please,
which way I ought to go from here?"
"That depends a good deal on where you want to get to,"
said the Cheshire Cat.
"I don't much care where –"said Alice.
"Then it doesn't matter which way you go", said the Cat.
"-so long as I get somewhere,"
Alice added as an explanation.
"Oh, you're sure to do that," said the Cat,
"if you only walk long enough."
Lewis Carroll, Alice's Adventures in Wonderland

Now we get to more practical stuff. With all the tools you already learnt you will be able to design the life you want and create your luck in whatever field of activity you choose.

Take a blank piece of paper and write everything you ever wanted to do in your life and still do. Anything – from jumping out of an aeroplane with a parachute to learning to play the piano and conquer Everest. They don't have to be grand and big. Think of small things like visiting that gallery or watching that DVD a friend recommended 3 years ago. Take your time, walk around, sit down again and write as many things as possible. Do not read any further until you do that! You can write them here.

Now look at your list. It is OK if you forgot something. You can add it to your list any time. Now put a number next to each goal according to its importance to you.

Now you can decide when you want these things to happen. You can choose either the deductive way (starting from longer term goals and then narrowing the down to shorter periods of time) or inductive (the opposite). Whatever is easier for you. For example:

Within Next 10 years:

Within Next 3 years:

Within next year:

Within 6 months:

This month:

Month 2:

Month 3:

Month 4:

Month 5:

Month 6:

This is the most important exercise ever - really think through it. You are programming your life now. You might forget about what you planned today, because I don't tell to stick to your original plan or die! You might have to readjust it or completely change it a few times. But you will be amazed when you look at it in 10 years time! Because very likely you will accomplish some things on your list even if you forgot about your planning. Some goals will look ridiculous to you as you will grow by that time and realize that buying a second Ferrari was really unnecessary. Or devoting your whole life to build your muscles to get that exposure in GQ was not a very good idea at the end of the day. You can always come back to your goals and check if something already changed in your plan. I do it as much as I feel I should – sometimes it happens every month and then for a year I don't touch it. As a time frame you can start with any number of years. Make it as realistic and achievable as possible, although it is good to stretch yourself a little bit. Remember if you put the bar high enough you have a bigger potential compared to if you put it lower and it won't be challenging enough for you in this case.

Take as much time as you want. You probably don't need to create anything, because it is already in your mind! All you need is to put it down on paper. Go on now!

Now we are getting closer to the core. Take one of your goals - any one. It can be something you want to happen next month or in any foreseeable future. Write it down in the present tense but with a future date. Think of something what should happen in order for you to know you have achieved it. For example:

It is now 12th of May 2010 and I am standing on a stage with 2 thousand people giving me a standing ovation. They are excited and can't wait for my presentation to begin. I am feeling confident and relaxed. I am ready to start my presentation on How to Change your Life in 3 Months and I have so much to tell.

Or:

It is 5th of September 2011 and I am driving along the coast of San-Francisco in my new Porsche and so on.

Make it as detailed as possible. Imagine the things you are going to see; hear the sounds and feel the feelings. Make the picture as bright as possible, if it is black and white make it colourful, if it is small make it really big and close.

Now shut your eyes and dissociate yourself from the picture —look at it as a photo of you or a film, so you can see yourself in it. Take the picture in your hands and rise up in the air. Imagine flying high up in the sky and higher than that until you can only see a line down below you – your time stream. In front of you is your future and behind you is your past. Imagine being just above Now and then flying into the future above the stream towards the date you put for your goal. Here it is — 12th of May 2010 or whatever date you have in your mind. Look at your picture again and energize it either with a thought or ha breath (whatever is strong enough for you) and drop the picture right above that date in the future. Now see how your future brightens up because of the goal you set. The time stream line becomes neon blue and lightens the space around it. Now look back. Your past has changed as well. In order to achieve your goal, things readjusted just so you can achieve it easily. Now fly back to Now and slowly get back into the room. Open your eyes.

The process you have just done is called Strategic Visioning. You can do it with all your goals. It is very individual and some people will find this process very useful. For others it is enough just to think about it. Whatever works for you, use it. Now you can practise it yourself.

_____

_____

_____

_____

_____

_____

_____

_____

_____

_____

_____

_____

_____

_____

_____

_____

_____

_____

_____

_____

_____

Now the last but not the least thing. On order to achieve your goals you need to realign them with your values. We have already talked about values. Just to remind you, values are things that are important to you. We live according to our values, make decisions, buy a car and marry. If my value number one is freedom and my friend's one is security, who do you think is more eager to create a family now? Or who is travelling the world with a backpack or who is working in the same company for the last 10 years? This is a bit straightforward and I am not saying one is better than another, but it is values which determine our way of life. For example if your most important value is freedom again and one of your goals is to create a family in 5 years time – then you will have to realign your values by that time, otherwise it just might not happen because it contradicts your plan!

Now take a few minutes and write down all things that are important to you. Try to see the difference between "means" and actual values. For example you can put down money as your value, but then why do you want money? Is it because you want to travel? Or buy a house? Then, why do you need the house? Is it to feel secure? Or comfortable? So probably your real value in this case would be comfort or security. Write as many as you can until you stop. Then give it another go, you might add a few more and then you come to the point you can't add any more, stop. If something comes up later, just add it to the list, but don't spend a lot of time on that.

Usually the list of people's values would look like this:

1. Family.

2. Friends.

3. Power.

4. Financial freedom/stability.

5. Honesty.

6. Communication.

7. Success.

It can be any order, just jot them down.

Now put a number next to each value according to it importance to you.   For example:

1. Financial freedom/stability

2. Friends.

3. Family.

4. Communication.

5. Honesty.

6. Power.

7. Success.

Now your list looks different. Try to do it on the same page, so you can see a difference. This is for your own reference. Now that you know what your values are, you can think what values should a person have in order to achieve those goals you wrote down before? If you are happy with what you have, we can move on to the next stage. If there are loud disagreements between your goals and values I would suggest you either speak about it with somebody you trust or even get professional advice from a life coach. Unfortunately we can't cover everything in this book and it can be a very personal process.

Now it is time to move on to the next chapter and look at how we are going with time and how we are actually good at organizing things and making them happen.

3.2. Going with time. Planning.

Understanding time.

"Don't say you don't have enough time. You have exactly the same number of hours that were given to Helen Keller, Pasteur, Michelangelo, Mother Teresa, Leonardo da Vinci, Thomas Jefferson, and Albert Einstein."

H. Jackson Brown

"The bad news is time flies.
The good news is you're the pilot."

Michael Altshuler

Our attitudes to time are constantly changing. Many of these changes are due to the advent of new technology, which affects our work, travel and communication. The Internet, e-mail, mobile phones have made the exchange of information almost instantaneous. Travel, especially over long distances, has become faster and more affordable. The increase in options available has made it possible for us to do more in a day, but also increased the pressure on our time. This makes it all the more important to use time in the most efficient way.

In this chapter I want you become aware of how you use your time. You can learn how to organize, prioritize and succeed in planning your daily life. Your time within your very individual schedule and rhythm will start working for you, instead of running ahead of you or lagging behind. Once you learn how to walk "with" time, you will realize that you can control it and use it to your advantage.

First, we are going to do one of my favourite exercises. You can use the space down below or you can practice first somewhere else. You can look at the example of Helen. Helen's problem is that she can never find time for her hobby – painting. She goes to University every day and she has a part-time job in the evening. But she feels that she still can keep on enjoying things she loves. All she needs to do is to become aware how she really spends her time and she can get more out of it.

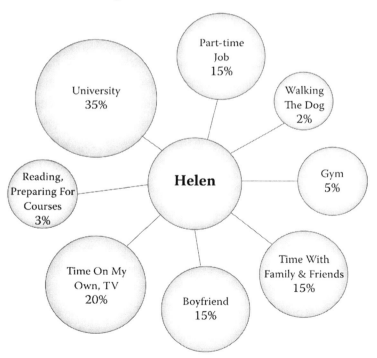

After looking at Helen's time chart, create one for yourself. Next to each activity you do, put a certain percentage – the share of your overall time you spend on this task. Don't spend too much time on it, figures are only approximate, it is not just the exact time you spent, it is also how much time you feel you spend.

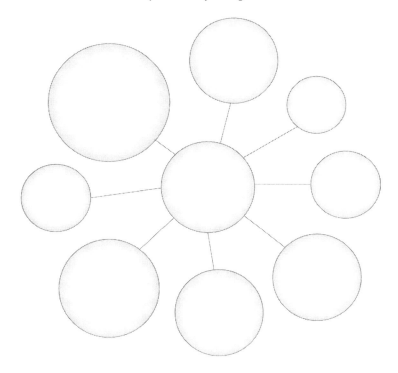

Good, once you finish the task, have a look at what your day usually looks like. Are you happy with that? Do you find enough time to do things you really love doing? Is there anything you would like to change? Maybe you want to spend less time on some activities, eliminate some or add a few more. Go on, open your mind, create your perfect day. Make it exciting, a day to look forward to every morning you wake up, fill it with balanced activities of work and pleasure. And just imagine how your life will change and how wonderful it is going to be once you start living your new plan. Remember, you can always readjust it. Your life in a few months time will be different from your life today, so it is good to review your plan from time to time. I do it as often as I need to, but usually it is every few months and it happens when I feel I could find a better use for my time.

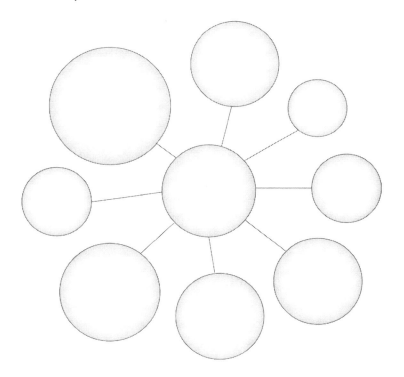

Comments:

_____

_____

_____

_____

_____

_____

_____

_____

_____

_____

Keeping a time log.

Maintaining a daily log of how much time you spend on particular activities is fundamental to managing your time more effectively.

Compile a simple time log by dividing your day into 30-minute chunks and recording exactly how you spend your time. This can be an additional help to determine how much time you spend on useful and unnecessary tasks.

Few of us will readily admit that large parts of our working day are wasted. It is very easy to spend too much time on routine things, such as reading mail, at the expense of high priority, productive tasks.

How do you divide up your day at the moment? Do

you prioritize your work so that you tackle important and urgent projects first? Or do you concentrate on completing enjoyable tasks first? Are you distracted by phone calls or do you have a system for dealing with them? Do you waste a lot of time?

Well, you cannot decide what to deal with today unless you know where you want to be tomorrow. Any plan to improve your use of time depends on being clear about your goals. As you have already set your goals, now you can just write them starting with ones that are high priority and dividing them into short, medium and long term. Also, you can divide them into personal and professional. Each goal on your list should involve the successful completion of a number of tasks. Decide which tasks are more important and need urgent attention.

Going With Time

_____

_____

_____

_____

_____

_____

_____

_____

_____

_____

_____

_____

_____

_____

_____

_____

    Priorities can change all the time because we receive information all the time, whether from the Internet, the telephone, or any other source. New information may change a task's importance or urgency, so you have to reassess your list of priorities.

Being Realistic

There are few things more stressful than exaggerated expectations, so be realistic about what you can achieve in a given period of time. Also you need some time to yourself - time to collect your thoughts, assess priorities, and concentrate on high-priority tasks.

Work Patterns.

Everybody has a natural daily rhythm to their energy patterns, rising to peaks of mental and physical performance and then experiencing troughs of low energy. Become familiar with your personal rhythm so that you can work with it rather than against it.

Using Time Planners.

Keeping a reliable and precise record of forthcoming events, appointments and obligations is crucial for efficient time management. There are many different types of planner available, so shop around to find the one that suits your needs best. It could be a standard diary, a personal organizer, or maybe an electronic planner. I find it easy to use a normal diary.

Doing things we don't enjoy.

Some things we just hate doing, but they still have to be done. Try to do a difficult job when you are in a positive frame of mind. Do not put it off until the end of the day, when you may be tired, or wait until just before the deadline.

Thinking positively.

Time can sail past for some people and drag for others. Which of the two applies to you depends mostly on your attitude. Use the power of positive thinking to make your plans successful, and that will change the whole experience.

What is it really all about? My philosophy.

We have been talking a lot about how to organize our time and to make the best of it, but we should not forget all this will never work if we don't have a grander purpose behind it. Why are we doing all this? Do we really want to achieve what we put down on paper? Are we doing that for ourselves or because somebody else wants us to do it? Because if you are really doing in life what you enjoy doing you will not waste a minute. So think twice before making plans you have no desire to realize. We always have a choice and sometimes things do not appear as they really are. Struggling and working long hours does not mean success. The trick is to be in the right place at the right time. And it can't be easier when we are in perfect balance with the universe and ourselves.

The value of time.

A businessman had amassed a fortune that amounted to three million gold dollars. He decided that he would take a year off from work and live in the kind of luxury that his wealth allowed him.

But no sooner had he made this decision than the Angel of Death beckoned him.

The man, who was a skilful negotiator, tried every argument he could think of to dissuade the Angel and to buy himself more time. But the Angel of Death was adamant; the man's time had come.

In final desperation, the rich man made the Angel an offer. "Give me three more days of life and I will give you a third of my wealth, a million gold dollars."

The Angel refused.

"Give me two more days of life and I will give you two thirds of my wealth, two million gold dollars."

The Angel again refused.

"Give me one more day of life, to enjoy this beautiful and bountiful planet, and to spend a little time with my family who I have neglected for too long, and I will give you all my wealth. Three million gold dollars."

But the Angel could not be persuaded.

Finally, the man asked if the Angel would just grant him a little time to write a short paragraph. And this wish was granted.

Make good use of your time on earth, he wrote. I could not buy even one hour of life for three million gold dollars. Be sure to know in your heart what things in your life are of true value, and place your attention there.

(Primary source: Idries Shah, The Way of the Sufi.)

3.3. Positive thinking. Focusing.

Positive thinking is essential in order to achieve your goals. You have to believe in yourself and build self-confidence. The following rules will help you in doing so.

- Formulate your positive outcome; picture it in your mind. Make this picture "alive" in your mind, enhance the colours and sounds, breathe some energy into it. Our mind always tries to develop the picture, so it is very important you only hold positive images, because you will get what you expect. Even if things are going really badly at the moment always hold onto your positive picture.

- Whenever a negative thought comes to mind, deliberately cancel it with a positive thought.

- Do not fear and create obstacles in your mind, minimise thinking of problems - difficulties must be dealt with whenever they come up, but don't create them before.

- Do not look at other people and try to copy them. Nobody can be as efficient as you can, trust in your own powers.

- Learn about the subject you are interested in, get professional advice.

- Remind yourself that everything happens for a reason and there are no coincidences. Accept the situation, do what you can do and leave things you can't deal with behind.

- Ask if you have questions and the answer will come to you, sometimes from an unexpected source.

- Trust yourself and your inner powers.

Once you set up your goals and gain the confidence you need, the next step would be to put your mind at peace. People can worry and laugh at the same problems. The essence of the secret lies in a change of mental attitude. Although changing thoughts requires effort it is still easier to make a change than to continue living as you are. The stressful life is a difficult one, the life of inner peace, filled with purpose and balance is the easiest way of existence.

Start each day with peaceful and contented thoughts and happy attitudes and your days will be pleasant and successful. Watch the way you talk, because it can be crucial which words you use. Refrain from using any negative expressions, as these tend to produce worry and tension.

The words we speak have direct effect on our thoughts and therefore reactions. Sometimes the best way is to say nothing. It is very useful to have at least fifteen minutes on your own. We all need some time when we can just be in silence and can rejuvenate our energy. When you are alone, make yourself comfortable and relax. It is great if you have a garden or can go to the park or to the beach.

Nature helps you to calm down and get closer to your true self.

Once your mind is at peace you will feel that flow of positive energy inside you. Keeping your energy high is essential to stay in a positive attitude. Some people get tired just because they are not interested in anything. Get engaged with something you really love. Always find time for your hobbies. Enthusiastic people are always positive!

Another factor is to stay happy. Sometimes it is fine to sulk a little bit, but ensure inside you are absolutely content. We do get irritated sometimes and it is OK to complain about things from time to time, but you can do it in a positive way and actually make fun of it! But stay happy inside. It is raining outside, great! Imagine how many wonderful things you can do at home, and it gets so fresh and clean after rain. Or maybe because of this rain you are missing a barbecue party you were so looking forward to? Well, nothing happens without a reason, as you know. Maybe if you did go this time you would stumble across somebody you didn't want to meet or something unpleasant would happen. Or maybe staying at home will make you available for something that will change your life, or maybe this is the perfect day to have some time on your own or spend it with a loved one?

Here are a few pieces of advice, which will help you eliminate worry from your life.

- Relax. Sit down in your chair or lie on the bed and close your eyes. Start relaxation from your toes and proceed to the top of your head.

- Think of a beautiful calm lake with a placid surface. Imagine your mind is as calm.

- Practise saying something positive concerning everything about which you have been thinking negatively. For example, instead of saying: "It is going to be a miserable day today," say something like: "It is going to be a glorious day!"

Once your attitude is right, it is time to get your focus right. Always aim for the best. We all deserve the best things in life, so why not set your bar higher and make it more challenging and therefore rewarding? We attract what we focus on and there is no limit to our powers.

Another important thing is how we relate to what we call "problems". You can call it an obstacle, a mistake, a disastrous event, unfortunate circumstances. But you would already start seeing a difference if you start calling them challenges, or experience, or feedback. What is a problem and how do we know we have one? Do we like blaming other people and prefer feeling guilty? Because neither is really right. When we do have a problem, are we focusing on the problem or on the solution? Here are a few methods for solving a problem.

- Believe that for every problem there is a solution.

- Keep calm and try to relax your brain from any tension. It cannot operate efficiently under stress and tension blocks the flow of thought power.

- Change your attitude towards the event. Ask yourself – is it really a problem? How can I use it to my advantage?

- Don't dwell on it for ages; if we try to force the solution, it won't make the answer to come quicker. Be patient, allow it some time. Keep you mind open and relaxed and it will come to you.

- Write down all the facts, pros and cons. This will clarify your thinking and the problem will become objective, not subjective.

- Ask the Universe for help and guidance.

- Trust your inner feelings and intuition; we are not given any challenges we can't overcome.

Now, when we are focused and worry free, we are going to look at something that some people don't feel comfortable about. It is about getting people to like you and to be able to communicate. I don't mean public speaking, lots of people fear speaking in front of a crowd, but still many of us don't know how to communicate simple ideas to people around us and make our friends and colleagues listen to us. A person would only listen to you if either you are an interesting person or you have something important to say. Of course they may listen to you because they feel they obliged to or scared, but that is not what you really want.

To create amazing relationships and be admired is not

something that comes exclusively from your charisma. This is something you can learn and start using in your life today.

Here are a few principles that will undoubtedly make you stand out of the crowd and make people listen to you.

- Learn to remember names. Our names are most important words to us. We feel significant if somebody who just met us remembers our name. This is as important for every day communications as for business ones. Write it down on a piece of paper or in your telephone. Do it for all people you meet, whether it is an estate agent you will have to contact again or the colleague sitting on the other side of the office. It is not an easy one, I would say. We always tend to focus on the content rather than context. Only by practising it can you train your memory and be good at it, unless you have a natural talent.

- Another thing that is crucially important is a person's birthday. This is obviously more personal. Try to be one of the first next time to congratulate your friend or especially somebody you don't see a lot. They will never forget it.

- Be an easygoing person, somebody to be fun with. The only way to do so is to be yourself, natural and open. We all like people like that. A superficial and arrogant person can never be the heart of a group.

- Unless it is your close friend, do not complain and blame anybody for anything. Instead, if you have to mention somebody else, say something nice about that person and be sincere.

- Don't give promises, but if you do say you are going to do something – do that promptly. If something changes and you are unable to deliver - let the person know as soon as possible. A responsible person is always a head taller in the crowd. If people know they can rely on you, they will make themselves available in case you ever need them.

- Don't be egoistical and argumentative. I know it is so tempting to show you know it all. Being naturally humble will make people admire you. And wise people do not argue or they make themselves fools.

- Become an interesting person, so you draw people to you, because they will love the fact being associated with you and getting value from being in your presence.

- Sincerely become interested in other people, practise liking them until you do so genuinely.

- Treat everybody the same way, don't generalise people or practise any division like nationalism or racism.

- Never miss an opportunity to say a word of

congratulation upon anyone's achievement, or express sympathy in sorrow or disappointment.

- Be strong and confident and people won't be able to resist you.

- Be clear and concise, nobody likes mixed messages. Honesty is another virtue if you want to get people to like you.

- Be available and generous. Sometimes a few minutes spent with somebody can change his whole life and yours.

- Give strength to people and they will give affection to you.

There is nothing new in these rules and you may have heard them all before. So there is no secret in becoming a likeable person. The best way is to get these principles to become your habit. Sometimes it is very useful to talk to your close friends and ask them for advice on what you can work on in your character. You can get really interesting feedback. Don't be ashamed of doing that – you will only feel more connected to each other and if not them, who else will tell you?

On the pages below write down what you think you are already good at (you can use the principles above, for example: I am good at remembering names, I am fun to be with, I am confident and a supportive friend. But I really need to work on integrity and being selfish from time to time. Also I need to be careful with what I say, so I don't hurt people I love.)

I am good at:

_____

_____

_____

_____

_____

_____

_____

_____

_____

I need to work on:

_____

_____

_____

_____

_____

_____

_____

_____

_____

People love me for:

_____

_____

_____

_____

_____

_____

_____

_____

_____

I can become even more successful in communicating if:

_____

_____

_____

_____

_____

_____

_____

_____

_____

3.4. Balancing emotions. Getting rid of negative beliefs and decisions.

We all feel frustrated or upset from time to time. And I don't think we should try to completely eliminate pain from our life —first, it would be impossible; second, pain is given to us for protection. You have probably heard the stories of people who suffer a sort of disease when they stop feeling pain in their limbs. Eventually they start neglecting these parts of their body and therefore lose them due to infection or other damage and then die. They call them lepers in India.

So sulking can be fine from time to time, it causes us to think about things, reflect on life, and if we don't go too far and cause real harm to ourselves and those around us, it is fine. We still want to be considered happy people, because it is so much fun to be around people who beam with joy and success. And we probably try to avoid friends who are always complaining. Do you know people like this?

But sometimes being down can get to be a habit and we might even enjoy the attention and the fact people constantly feel sorry for us. We make it our way of life and become "a poor George" or "poor Mary". I believe you are not one of those people, but you might know someone.

It's natural to believe that external events upset you. When you are mad at someone, you automatically make him or her the cause of your bad feelings. You say, "You are annoying me! You are getting on my nerves." When you think like this, you are actually fooling yourself because other people cannot make you angry.

Yes, you heard me right. A pushy teenager can jump a queue in front of you at the movie theatre, your business partner can screw you out of your share in a profitable business, your boyfriend can behave selfishly and uncaring toward you and forget about an important anniversary. No matter how outrageous and unfair others might appear to you, they do not, never did, and never will upset you. The bitter truth is that you are the one who is creating every drop of the feelings you experience, no matter what.

It might be difficult to accept, but if we really have a habit of doing that.

Imagine two different people were robbed while shopping in a busy shopping mall. They both lost their wallets with all their credit cards and some cash as well. What can be more annoying? (Actually thinking of something much worse that happened to you, will make you feel much better.)

So, John and Peter both lost their wallets. And they just started shopping, so they have to change all their plans as well! Peter completely lost it. He started panicking and calling his wife, then he realised he needed to cancel his cards and he was very rude to the bank manager. His lost his temper for the next few days and decided that from now on his wife was going to do all the shopping, because he was so "absent minded".

John obviously could have done the same thing, but he decided to keep things cool this time. He informed the police promptly and called the bank to cancel his cards. Then he went to the bank, took out some cash and continued shopping. Not that he wasn't upset at all, he found it very annoying as well, but he realised it is not the worst thing that could happen and it's not worth getting a heart attack over.

There are obviously different scenarios in the middle. The point is these situations happen and will continue to happen in our life. Sometimes we will have no control over them. Therefore we might accept the situation and think about why it happened to us and what lesson we can learn from it. Maybe we can use it to our advantage in some way?

I simply have to mention what happened to very recently. I was finishing the last pages of the first draft of this book, and I should add it's been a very busy and stressful time for me in the last month or so. I was preparing for an exam, started to be really involved in my city job, there were some relationship and family issues as well. So, it is 11 pm and I finish my last sentence. But this time I can hardly keep my eyes open and all I can think of is that I need to set my alarm clock for 5.30 as usual to go to work.

I save my file, too tired even to really be happy about the work I've completed. Then I thought I'd better back it up, sending it to my other laptop. But the file is not there. It is just gone. All I have is work I have done before last week. And the last seven chapters are missing. Still quite confident it should be somewhere on a hard disk I go to bed and decide to show it to the IT guy at work. Next morning it is the only thing I can think about. I take some orders from the clients, but I can't concentrate. For some reason the computer didn't save the file so we were unable to recover it. I was quite devastated; all my work for the last week was gone, hours and hours of reading, typing and thinking. Somehow I was calm inside and the solution came quickly. I asked my boss to let me go till the end of the week and he did. Yes, I had to do it all again, but it didn't put me off. For some reason I thought it's for the best: I will create a better book, I will use this time off to relax and get the energy, I will be able to go out with my boyfriend and celebrate when I finish the writing. (Before this happened I had plans to go to the office party that evening.)

All these things would be impossible if it didn't happen to me! I want to emphasize, it is not that I would rather it happen to me than not, but because it already happened and I cannot do anything about it, I accept the situation the way it is and find all the positive things about it.

Apart from your attitude there are a few other tools you can use to balance your emotions and live a more content and fulfilled life. Those are your beliefs and the decisions you make.

Beliefs are your convictions, those things you consider true. If you believe you can learn anything that you put your mind to, regardless of your age, your experiences are going to be very different from those people who believe they are not very smart and couldn't possibly learn something new. The beliefs that don't serve you can narrow your possibilities tremendously. On the other hand, when transformed, beliefs can give you wings to your potential and allow you to soar to new heights.

A dear friend of mine truly believed that the only way she could be happy and achieve success was to move abroad. For four years in a row she was living in different parts of the world: USA, England, Germany, but she was content enough to stay there for more than a year. After coming back to Russia she fell into a depression for a few months, at the same time trying desperately to organize a trip somewhere else, "just not to stay here". Summer came and things suddenly changed. She found a new job, met a nice guy and actually is planning to stay here until something better comes up. She realized that limiting herself, in this case geographically, not only made her unhappy and limited her choices, but also made her ill.

In NLP we use different tools to obliterate negative emotions or get rid of negative beliefs. If you are really interested and want to see an instant change in your attitude you should talk to an expert, an NLP practitioner. At the same time you have already got enough tools to do it on your own. You can decide which beliefs actually harm you (I am not good enough, I am too slow, I am not smart, rich, attractive... and so on) and you can work on those by realising that we are all unique and have different purposes in our lives. That no one on this planet is exactly like you and we have a huge potential and undiscovered treasure within us. That we are all loved by the Universe and we can achieve anything we want.

All you need to do is to take a decision. Decisions are one of the major filters of our experience. Throughout your life you make decisions, both consciously and unconsciously. Someone who decides early in life that he or she will one day become President of the United States of America will have a different experience of life than someone who decides that he or she will never amount to anything. We shape our destiny with every decision we make. Our life today is the result of the decisions we made yesterday.

Before we move on to the next chapter and start talking about change and transformation, I want you to do a small exercise. Write down below your negative beliefs and decisions and how you think your life will change if you get rid of them. Then, imagine that somebody is defending you, like your barrister in court (you can do it yourself or ask a friend).

For example:

My negative belief:

I am shy and reserved. I am scared of talking in public.

__If I got rid of this belief__ my life would change

dramatically. My colleagues will respect me more. I will become more popular and make new friends. It will be easier for me to get new clients and therefore make more money. My life is going to be more fun. People will listen to me.

Defence: I know I can give a small talk if I am well prepared. People quite like me anyway. I am an interesting person and I have got a lot to say.

My negative decision:

I decided that I am not good enough (not as good as my brother).

If I get rid of this decision I will feel more confident and will love myself for who I am and what I achieved.

Defence: I am good at so many things actually. I was the best swimmer at school. I love my job and my colleagues and friends think I am a fun person to be with. I am in a good health...and so on.

My negative belief:

_____

_____

_____

If I got rid of that belief:

_____

_____

_____

Defence:

_____

_____

_____

_____

My negative decision:

_____

_____

_____

If I got rid of that decision:

_____

_____

_____

_____

Defence:

_____

_____

_____

3.5. Change and transition. (Transformation)

"Variety's the very spice of life,
That gives it all its flavour."
William Cowper 1731-1800: The Task (1785)

"Everything flows and nothing stays...
You can't step twice into the same river."
Heraclitus c.540-480 BC: Plato Cratylus.

"Change is not made without inconvenience,
even from worse to better."
Samuel Johnson 1709-84:
A Dictionary of the English Language (1755)

Now that we have learned all these tools and we feel we are ready to start living a new life, life with a purpose and new possibilities, we should ask ourselves: are we ready to accept all those changes coming into our life? People tend to be cautious of anything new, some even fear changes. It is easy to get comfortable and adapt to the situation even if we know we could do better than that. So change takes you out of your comfort zone, makes you think harder, work harder and take different kinds of decisions. With all that come new experiences and new exciting opportunities. Usually people wait in their life situation until the threshold, when they simply cannot bear it any more. Then they feel like they have no choice but to take a new decision. It is called moving away from pain.

We certainly don't have to wait that long. We always have options, even if sometimes we don't see them straight away. Making this leap in uncertainty takes a lot of courage, but at the end of the day, it is essential. Life is based on change. The second we are born, we start changing. We never stop renewing our body cells and getting rid of the old ones. This is a very slow process, so invisible for us. If we don't feed our mind with new knowledge it will degrade. We are in a constant search for growth and expansion. The second we give up — the reverse process starts —we grow old and die.

If we don't take control and do it, circumstances will do it for us. Learn to love change. Just because we don't know what it brings to us, if we are daring enough to accept it, it will never disappoint us. Change is the catalyst that creates the reactions in life. We can only get to know this world and make our life richer by daring and trying new things. Of course, I don't mean we have to jump from one thing to another all the time, changing jobs, countries or girlfriends for the sake of experience. But at some point in life, we know it is around the corner and start feeling doubtful and scared. At this moment I would like to remind you that this change wasn't made yesterday, but, perhaps, you made yourself available and sent an unconscious thought into the Universe. Now do you feel unsure, or are you really not?

Maybe a part of you craves it and is so excited that it is scared. Another part of you thinks of the pain and inconvenience change can bring, and a comfortable life now, though pretty boring and purposeless. So I will assume you know the answer better than anybody else.

If you think you are one of those people who come to the crossroads, but pretty sure know which road they are going to take (even if they can't confess it to themselves), I dare you to write down the changes you are going to face. It's that simple. Sometimes saying something or putting it on paper can make a whole new difference. I would suggest you say, "I decide to" instead of "I want to", because it will be much stronger in this case. For example:

"I decide to start exercising and watch my diet. I decide to be healthy and fit".

Or:

"I decide to break off this relationship, because there are not enough reasons to be together any more and give myself and the other person the opportunity to move on."

3.6. Going with the flow. Synchronicity.

What is it that makes us happy? What exactly are we doing when we feel enjoyment or fulfilment?

There was a research study on a group of people. They were required to write down exactly what they were doing and the feelings that the activity produced. The discovery was that the best moments didn't happen by chance, according to the whim of external events, but could reasonably be predicted to occur when a specific activity was undertaken. The activities described as being of highest value, which when undertaken banished worry or thoughts of other things, were dubbed "optimal experiences" or simply "flow."

People in the state of flow feel that they are engaged in something purposeful and creative; athletes call it "being in the zone", other people call it "ecstasy" or simply the experiences that make time stand still.

In the larger context, flow is feeling connected. It is living every day of your life, knowing "you will get there". It is hearing the answers before you finish the question, being in the right place at the right time.

Sometimes we feel disconnected for a while and it is fine as long as we charge our batteries on time.

Living in a big city like London with all its business, noise and pressure makes it essential for me to go away from time to time and immerse myself in nature. At the same time, London is a source of energy, but it is a different kind of energy. So it is not actually where you are and what are you doing, but how you manage to keep the balance between work and pleasure.

I remember just a few months ago I could lie in bed as long as I wanted to. I would go to the gym every day, have a few meetings during the day and then go to the cinema in the evening. I would go travelling a few times a month and go to all sorts of seminars in different countries. Then I suddenly found myself waking up at 5.30 every day, taking a tube to the city, throwing myself into the trading floor buzz and then would have more meetings after work. But I must confess I still love it. All those years of studying, self-development, travelling and business ventures started to pay off.

I knew the change was coming and I embraced it. And we are never given more to cope with than we can handle. I believe everything in our life has a purpose, we come across opportunities every day and we can feel good any time. You already have all the tools you need to feel the same way.

Even the most stubborn and sceptical of us must admit that there is more to us than just a body. This flow goes through us and around us. It has no beginning or end.

You are almost ready now for the journey of self-discovery. What is it like for you when you feel in the flow?

Going In The Flow

3.7. Living it.

Here you are, ready to move to the next stage, to conquer the world, to find the Treasure. Perhaps you didn't realise but the process has begun some time ago. How is it going to be for you? I don't know. You way is different to mine. Living the principles you read in this book will definitely guide you to the top of your mountain. The choice is yours.

As I mentioned before, living your purpose, feeling connected and achieving your goals doesn't mean your life is always going to be a bed of roses. It will just change the way you look at things, what you will see behind those experiences, how you are going to react in those circumstances.

If you take these lessons on board, you probably won't go back to your past way of thinking and you can now expect your life to change significantly. I will leave you now with your thoughts.

Conclusion.

This book is not a shortcut, but a map and you can choose any way to get to your treasure. I had to go through the journey of self-discovery myself. My resources were hundreds of books, various people and experiences, travelling, reflection. I found some of my treasure, and this book is a part of it. There is still a lot more to discover. I know it will take a lifetime.

I wish you well on your journey. Open your heart and let the treasure shine through you to light up the whole world.

Life is like climbing a mountain. The higher we get, the further is the horizon. Our path is full of surprises and adventures. We walk up the path and enjoy beautiful scenery, the singing of birds, the fresh breeze in the air and the aroma of pine trees. We meet other strangers like us, some people just pass by, others keep us company for a while and then we continue, each on our own way. We walk and walk, cheerfully and full of hope. Sometimes we lose our footing and slither down, but our will and determination help us to get to the very top. Further and higher, until there is only the endless blue sky. We reach our goal, plant our flag. We choose our mountain ourselves. On the top we stop and turn around to contemplate the most amazing view we've ever seen. We look at the difficult path we just travelled – there was so much in our way –steep rocks and fast springs, deep cracks and holes, wild animals, severe winds and pouring rain. Now the sun is shining and warming us up with its rays. We reflect on our journey. Maybe we chose the wrong mountain, maybe it was just a hill and the real mountain is still ahead. If we feel happy and peaceful in our heart we know we've reached our aim, mastered the Art of Life, found our Treasure.

Bibliography

Demartini, Dr. John F. *The Breakthrough Experience: A Revolutionary Approach to Personal Transformation.* Carlsbad, CA: Hay House, Inc., 2002.

McTaggart, Lynne. *The Field: The Quest for the Secret Force of the Universe.* New York: Harper Collins, 2002.

Berne, E. *Games People Play: The Psychology of Human Relationships,* London: Penguin, 1964.

Burns, D. *Feeling Good: The New Mood Therapy,* New York: William Morrow, 1980.

Csikszentmihalyi, M. *Creativity: Flow and the Psychology of Discovery and Invention,* New York: Harper Collins, 1996.

Gladwell, M. Blink. *The Power of Thinking without Thinking,* London: Penguin, 2005.

Maslow, A. *The Farther Reaches of Human Nature,* London: Penguin, 1976.

Carnegie, D. *How to Win Friends and Influence People,* New York: Pocket Books, 1994.

Chopra, D. *Ageless Body, Timeless Mind: A Practical Alternative to Growing Old,* London: Rider, 1993.

Chopra, D. *Kama Sutra: Including the Seven Spiritual Laws of Love,* London: Virgin Books, 2006.

McKenna, P. *I Can Make You Rich*, London: Bantam Press, 2007.

Grayling, A.C. *The Meaning of Things: Applying Philosophy to Life*, London: Phoenix, 2002.

Patmore, B. *Perfect Vision: Being the Best You Can Possibly Be*, Cambridge: Granta Editions, 1991.

Hawking, S. *A Brief History of Time: From the Big Bang to Black Holes*, London: Bantam Books, 1995.

Hoover, J. *Time Management: Set Priorities to Get the Right Things Done*, New York: Harper Collins, 2007.

Kranz, G. *Communicating Effectively: Write, Speak, and Present with Authority*, New York: Harper Collins, 2007

Hill, N. *Think and Grow Rich*, London: Vermilion, 2003.

Owen, N. *The Magic of Metaphor*, Wales; Crown House Publishing Ltd, 2001.

Covey, S. *The 7 Habits of Highly Effective People*, New York: Simon & Schuster, 1990.

Dyer, W. *Real Magic: Creating Miracles in Everyday Life*, New York: Harper Collins, 1993.

Emerson, R.W. *Self-Reliance and Other Essays*, Dover Publications, 1993.

Koch, R. *The 80/20 Principle: The Secret of Achieving More with Less*, London: Nicholas Brealey Publishing, 1998.

Gray, J. *Men Are from Mars, Women Are from Venus: A Practical Guide for Improving Communications and Getting What You Want in Your Relationships*, London: Harper Collins, 1992.

Hay, L. *You Can Heal Your Life*, Carlsbad CA: Hay House, 1999.

Peale, N.V. *The Power of Positive Thinking*, New York: Ballantine Books, 1996.

Peck, M.S. *The Road Less Travelled: A New Psychology Of Love, Traditional Values and Spiritual Growth*, London: Arrow Books, 1990.

Robbins, A. *Awaken the Giant Within*, New York: Simon& Schuster, 1993.

Byrne, Rhonda. *The Secret*, New York: Atria Books / Beyond Words, 2006.

Thomas, K. Kama Sutra: *The Ultimate Guide to the Secrets of Erotic Pleasure*, London: HarperElement, 2006.

Howard, C. *Turning Passions into Profits*, New Jersey: Wiley, 2004.

About the Author

Sofia Adamova, performance consultant, Director of Treasure Companies Ltd.

Sofia specializes in:

- strategic visioning planning,
- leadership development,
- executive coaching,
- communication,
- personal transformation.

Sofia works with entrepreneurs and senior executives within small to medium organizations and businesses. Her principal focus is helping individuals and teams produce exceptional results through relationships based on shared commitment to the purpose of the organization.

Sofia was born in a small town in the south of Russia in the family of educators. She studied International Economics and after graduating in 2004 she moved to London.

Sofia has always had the spirit of an entrepreneur and she was involved in the number of different ventures – from co-founding a company selling marketing space to Russian and former Soviet Union big cap companies to setting up her own fashion label.

Currently Sofia is working as a stockbroker and living in Chelsea.

www.thetreasurecompanies.co.uk
thetreasurecompanies@gmail.com

Lightning Source UK Ltd.
Milton Keynes UK
18 November 2009

146401UK00001B/16/P